Ruff Ruffman's
44 FAVORITE
Science Activities

CANDLEWICK
ENTERTAINMENT

CONTENTS

INTRODUCTION

GREETINGS, FETCHers!

You love science and I do, too! Welcome to my collection of favorite experiments and science activities. What's included, you ask? Totally AWESOME stuff: rocket ships; fizzy, foamy potions; a thrill-tastic roller coaster— even secret spy stuff like invisible ink *(shh)*! And TONS MORE! There are oodles of ways to use this book.

TAKE THE *FETCH!* CHALLENGE

Test your determination, daring, and intellect by taking the *FETCH!* challenge. Each experiment is worth a set number of Challenge Points. Add up all of your points for a Triumph Tally, and then see how you did at the end of the book. I triple-dog-dare you to do them all!

Challenge Points
15

START A *FETCH!* CLUB

What's more fun than doing science experiments? Starting a club to do them with friends! To get started, set a schedule and pick a meeting location. When the group is assembled, make a Challenge Points chart to keep track of everyone's score. Establish a Challenge Points goal for you and your friends to reach. For example, total the points of the five experiments you might plan to complete for a perfect score. At each meeting, after completing the day's experiment, update the Challenge Points chart with points earned by each member. If you wish, decorate a bulletin board with photos, the *FETCH!* Solve a Problem sign (p. 7), and your chart.

FETCH! LAB RULES

Scientists put safety first. Post these rules in your own laboratory, which can be set up in your kitchen or any space that has a table and a trash container. A sink is helpful, too.

1. Before beginning any experiment, ask a grown-up for permission. Get adult help with any experiment that has my red paw print, as it may involve heat, flame, or chemicals.

2. Read all the instructions before beginning an experiment. And before you start, make sure you have enough time to finish it.

3. Keep it clean. Wash your paws before and after experiments. Use clean containers, and when you're done, clean your area and all your materials.

4. Be sure to check with an adult before using any materials besides the ones listed.

5. Never touch electrical sockets, plugs, or wires.

6. Never taste or eat chemicals you're using for an experiment.

7. Label everything. Experiments might be ruined if you can't remember what's in each jar or the chemicals get mixed up.

8. Don't pour mixtures down the drain. Always throw them in the trash.

9. Never leave any project unattended unless it's safe to do so. You don't want your dog getting into it or your younger sibling mistaking a cup of solution for a drink.

10. Science is a blast. Enjoy yourself!

DAZZLE AT THE SCIENCE FAIR

Science fair coming up at school? No worries!
Everything you need to know about preparing
experiments for presentation IS RIGHT HERE!
Need a topic? Choose an experiment
based on what you love.
What are your hobbies?
What are you curious about?
Next, pose a question.
Specific, open-ended ones work best.
Most science fair projects are displayed on
three-paneled backboards. Make sure yours is neat
and well organized, with material that's short and to-the-point.

Abstract

Project Title

Conclusion

Question

Materials

Hypothesis

Procedure

Background Research

Results

Future Directions

Science Fair Tip

Throughout the book are "pawsome" tips on how to present your information.

Then it's time to practice. If you can explain your science fair project well to the judges, you boost your chances of winning. Write a short speech (under five minutes), and practice it until you feel comfortable. Talk slowly, smile, and remember: the judges are on your side!

And remember that it's OK if your prediction turns out to be false, as long as you used the scientific method. (More on that in a minute.) Maybe you'll come up with a new prediction and try, try again. Doing a science project isn't about getting one right answer. It's about exploring, discovering, working together, and having fun!

THE SCIENTIFIC METHOD

(AKA How to Solve a Problem *FETCH!*-Style)
For many experiments, you'll use what's called the scientific method. That's just a fancy-schmancy name for the problem-solving steps that scientists, engineers, and FETCHers use to tackle a challenge.

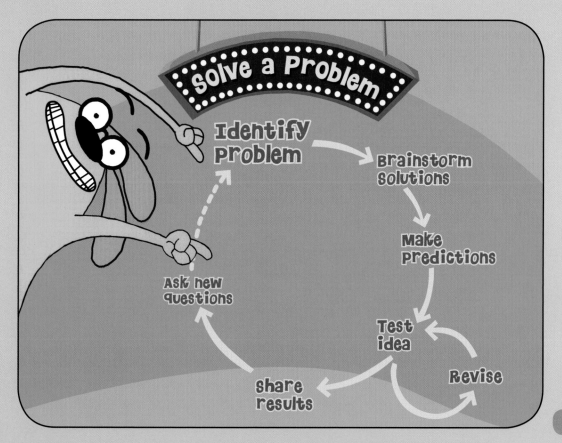

= easy

= moderately challenging

= challenging

FeTcH!

Refer to the experiment's bone count to see how easy or challenging it will be.

SAFETY TIP

• Before beginning any experiment, look for my red paw print to see if you'll need help from a grown-up.

YOUR MOST IMPORTANT TOOL

STOP! Before reading any further, go grab a notebook. I'll wait. . . .

Got one? Good. Scientists need to keep detailed notes of their experiments. Otherwise, how would they know what worked and what didn't?

In your lab notebook, you'll record the name and date of each experiment, your hypothesis, observations, materials, results, and other data. You can also include drawings, tables, charts, graphs— or, for inspiration, a photo of your science hero.

(Ahem. That's me, right?)

AB-RUFF-CA-DAB-RUFF!

You hear a lot about boy and girl wizards in books and movies. But never a word about dog wizards . . . until now! To work my magic, I'll need some truly bewitching potions. AB-RUFF-CA-DAB-RUFF! Try these chemistry experiments to conjure up concoctions worthy of a canine wizard.

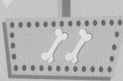

PENNY HOCUS-POCUS

If you don't have a magic wand to make dull pennies shine, can you make them sparkle with . . . ketchup? . . . baking soda? . . . or cola?

> If I had a penny for every time somebody asked for my world-famous orange-and-herring juice, I'd still be broke.

SAFETY TIPS

- Ask an adult for help!
- Keep mixtures away from clothes, eyes, and mouth.
- No tasting!

What You'll Need:

- 7 dull pennies • 6 cups • a spoon • 3 spoonfuls of household cleaner with ammonia
- 2 spoonfuls of baking soda mixed with some water • 3 spoonfuls of vinegar • 3 spoonfuls of lemon juice • 3 spoonfuls of cola • 3 spoonfuls of ketchup • 6 strips of pH paper (found at pool-supply stores and some drugstores) • a bowl or cup of water for rinsing • paper towels

What to Do:

1 PREPARE A DATA TABLE.

Copy the one on page 12 into your lab notebook.

2 SET UP THE PENNIES.

Line up the cups in front of the data table and put a penny in each cup. Place the extra penny on the sheet—it will be your control. You'll use it later to compare with the others.

3 ADD THE LIQUIDS.

In each cup, pour enough liquid to cover the penny:
(1) household cleaner, (2) baking soda and water, (3) vinegar, (4) lemon juice,
(5) cola, and (6) ketchup.

Let the pennies sit for at least five minutes.

4 MAKE A PREDICTION AND WRITE IT IN YOUR LAB NOTEBOOK.

Which liquids do you think will shine the pennies the best?

5 TEST FOR MORE INFORMATION.

While you wait, find out more about your liquids.
Using pH paper, discover if each is an acid or a base.

Dip one end of a pH paper strip in the first cup.
If it turns reddish, the liquid is an acid;
if it turns bluish-green,
the liquid is a base.

Place the strip on your data table and write down whether the
liquid is an acid or a base.

Repeat these steps with each liquid and fresh strips of pH paper.

6 CHECK THE PENNIES.

Use a spoon to remove the penny
from the first cup. Rinse it in water
and dry it. Then place it on the data
table. Repeat with the other pennies,
cleaning the spoon after each cup.
Keep your hands as clean as possible.

7 DRAW CONCLUSIONS.

Look at your control penny and compare
it to the others. How do the other pennies
look in comparison? Which liquids
shined the pennies the best?
Can you tell if one type of liquid —
acid or base — did the better job?

Data Table:

This is the sort of data table you can include in your lab notebook.
Copy this one to record your observations.

PENNY HOCUS-POCUS

Name: _____

	household cleaner	baking soda and water	vinegar	lemon juice	cola	ketchup
pH strip (put here)						
Acid or Base?						
Penny (put here)						

Place dull penny here for comparison. This is called the control.

FETCH! with Ruff Ruffman

CHEW ON THIS!

Pennies are made with copper. After they've been exposed to air for a while, a dull coating of copper and oxygen, called copper oxide, forms on them. When some acids (like the ones you used) come in contact with copper, there's a chemical reaction that dissolves the copper oxide, making the penny shiny again. But the bases you tested left the pennies looking dull. Bases don't cause a chemical reaction with copper (or any metal), so they can't dissolve copper oxide.

Science Fair Tip

Make a neater version of the data table shown to use in your display, and attach the pennies. Create a border out of penny-roll wrappers.

DIG DEEPER

SPEED CLEANING

Want to shine your pennies even faster? Add a spoonful of salt to vinegar or lemon juice. Swirl a penny around in the mix and watch it shine up before your eyes.

COPPER COATING

Use copper from pennies to coat another object. Put about ten dull pennies in a cup with a vinegar and salt mix. After a few minutes, remove the pennies, but keep the liquid. Add a paper clip. Wait about 10 minutes to a half hour. The copper oxide from the pennies will transfer to the paper clip, changing its color.

TEMPEST IN A TEACUP

It's hot! It's cold! It's bubbly! You won't believe the chemical reactions you can create in a cup!

SAFETY TIPS

- Ask an adult for help!
- Keep mixtures away from clothes, eyes, and mouth.
- No tasting!

What You'll Need:

- baking powder • baker's yeast • hydrogen peroxide • vinegar • 4 plastic cups
- 2 plastic spoons • paper towels

What to Do:

1 PREPARE A DATA TABLE.

Label each column with the contents of one cup, as below. Include two rows to observe the chemical reactions' occurrence and what they look like.

2 SET UP THE CUPS.

Add a spoonful of baking powder to two of the cups. Lable one BAKING POWDER AND HYDROGEN PEROXIDE. Label the other BAKING POWDER AND VINEGAR.

Add a spoonful of yeast to each of the two other cups. Label one YEAST AND HYDROGEN PEROXIDE. Label the other YEAST AND VINEGAR.

3 MAKE PREDICTIONS.

What do you think will happen when these substances are combined? Signs of a chemical reaction you may observe include heat, cold, and fizzing or bubbling.

4 TEST THE COMBINATIONS.

Add an inch or two of hydrogen peroxide to the cup marked BAKING POWDER AND HYDROGEN PEROXIDE. Pour carefully or use an eye-dropper. (Be sure to rinse it out between solutions.)

What do you notice? Did you see or feel any signs of a chemical reaction? Write down your observations.

5 TEST, OBSERVE, AND RECORD.

Now test the other three combinations, adding hydrogen peroxide and vinegar to the appropriate cups.

Write down your observations.

6 DRAW CONCLUSIONS.

Review the observations you recorded. Which combinations produced chemical reactions? How would you describe them? Did some last longer than others?

CHEW ON THIS!

Chemical reactions can produce brand-new substances. There are many clues that let you know a chemical reaction has taken place. In this activity, you witness changes in temperature (both hot and cold), as well as fizzing and bubbling. The fizzing and bubbling mean a gas is being produced. For example, mixing yeast and hydrogen peroxide forms water and oxygen (a gas), and mixing baking powder and vinegar produces carbon dioxide (also a gas).

DIG DEEPER

FANTASTIC FOAM

If you liked the fizzing and foaming in this experiment, you'll love what happens when you add a squirt of dish-washing soap to hydrogen peroxide and yeast.

Science Fair Tip

Take photos of the reactions you observe for a display.

10

POTION POWER

Water and oil don't mix. But watch what happens when you add the fizz factor! Double, double, toil and trouble . . .

SAFETY TIPS

• Ask an adult for help!
• Keep mixtures away from clothes, eyes, and mouth.
• No tasting!

What You'll Need:

• 4 clear plastic cups • vegetable oil • water • white vinegar • food coloring • fizzing antacid tablets • baking soda • paper towels

What to Do:

1 PREPARE A DATA TABLE.

Copy the one on page 18 into your lab notebook.

2 SET UP THE CUPS.

Line up the cups, and add about an inch or two of oil to each.

3 ADD THE OTHER LIQUIDS.

Add about an inch or two of water to two of the cups and label them OIL AND WATER.

Add about an inch or two of vinegar to the other two cups and label them OIL AND VINEGAR.

What do you notice about the oil, water, and vinegar? Record your observations in your lab notebook.

Add three drops of food coloring to each of the four cups. Do not stir. What do you observe now? Write down what you see.

4 MAKE A PREDICTION

Predict what will happen if you add a piece of the fizzy tablet to one cup of oil and water and a piece to one cup of oil and vinegar.

Predict what will happen if you add a spoonful of baking soda to the two remaining cups.

Write down your predictions in your lab notebook.

5 TEST THE CHEMICAL REACTIONS.

Add the fizzy tablet, and write or draw your observations in your lab notebook.

Add the baking soda, and describe or draw your observations in your lab notebook.

6 DRAW CONCLUSIONS.

You can tell that a chemical reaction has taken place if you see fizzing or bubbling. Describe what you see. Was there a chemical reaction in each cup?

BAKING SODA

CHEW ON THIS!

Oil and water don't mix, and neither do oil and vinegar—that's why they form separate layers of liquid. Oil is less dense than water or vinegar, so it floats on top. The fizzing tablets and the baking soda cause chemical reactions with water and vinegar in three of the cups, producing bubbles of carbon dioxide gas. Because gas is less dense than the liquids, the gas bubbles float to the top, bringing along some of the colored water or vinegar.

Science Fair Tip

Display "before" and "after" photos of your experiment, and perform it at the fair.

DIG DEEPER

DENSITY TOWER

Create colorful layers of liquids. Who knew that oil, water, and corn syrup could look so good? Add red food coloring to some corn syrup and blue to some water. Then pour some oil, the corn syrup, and the water into a clear glass, so they form layers with the densest on the bottom and the least dense on top. Predict the correct order to pour them in.

POTION POWER

FeTCH! with Ruff Ruffman

Name: _____

Line up your cups in front of each label. Make sure your mixtures match the labels. Describe (or draw) your observations.

Oil and Water & Fizzing Tablet	Oil and Water & Baking Soda	Oil and Vinegar & Fizzing Tablet	Oil and Vinegar & Baking Soda

IN THE DOGHOUSE

I run my insanely popular show from my state-of-the-art headquarters, otherwise known as my doghouse. From the outside, it's pretty much what you'd expect (a roof, four walls, a couple of worn-out squeaky toys), but inside, it's a different story. For one thing, it holds my Fetch 3000 — an amazing computer capable of tabulating scores, disposing of annoying cats, and blending the occasional smoothie.

But just how strong is my doghouse? Try these experiments to find out. (Oh, and can you make me one of those groovy lava lamps while you're at it? It would look great by my bark-o-lounger.)

10 CANINE HOUSE OF CARDS

Build a two-story building for Ruff out of index cards, using just one shape — a square, an arch, or a triangle. Then see if it can support the weight of a jumbo dog biscuit on top!

Build me a model of my new headquarters — and make sure there's a dog-bone statue on top. I want everyone to know that a dog runs the show!

What You'll Need:

• index cards • tape • large dog biscuits

What to Do:

1 MAKE THE SHAPES, AND PICK ONE TO BUILD WITH.

Tape together a square, an arch, and a triangle out of cards, and test each one for strength and stability. Push down on them and rock them side to side. Choose one shape to build with — the one you think will make the strongest, most stable structure. Be sure to follow the building rules below and on the next page.

To make the arch, overlap two cards about an inch at the top, then tape.

Shapes must be upright (see triangle at left), not on their side (at right).

BUILDING RULES

Build with one shape only.

Your building must be at least two stories high.

You cannot lay a shape on its side.

You can tape shapes together.

You can build a flat platform on top for the dog biscuit.

 BRAINSTORM SOME IDEAS.

What's the best way to build your two-story building? How wide should you make the base? What kind of surface or platform will be needed to support the dog biscuit?

 BUILD A TWO-STORY BUILDING.

Use tape and index cards to construct a building out of the shape you chose.

 TEST AND REDESIGN.

Can you place a dog biscuit on top without it falling off or toppling the building? Can your building support even more dog biscuits? If not, redesign. You can even start over using a different shape.

DRAW CONCLUSIONS.

Which shape was the strongest?

CHEW ON THIS!

The material that a building is made from—
wood, concrete, brick, or steel, for example—affects
how strong and stable it is. But the shapes used to build
a structure also help the structure support weight. In this activity,
you tested three commonly used architectural shapes: arches, squares, and triangles.
The material in this building activity (thin index cards) is weak, so you have to rely on
the shape to help provide strength. And, now that you've tried this out, you know which
shape is the strongest of them all!

WANTED: LAVA LAMP

Use your science skills to
make Ruff a lava lamp for
his doghouse.

Groovy, baby!

What You'll Need:

• a large clear plastic bottle with a cap • water • a funnel • vegetable oil • food coloring
• a fizzing antacid tablet • a flashlight (optional)

What to Do:

 1 BUILD YOUR LAVA LAMP.

Fill the bottle one-third with water.

Using the funnel, slowly pour the vegetable oil into the bottle until it's almost full.

After the oil and water have separated, add ten drops of food coloring.

Put the cap on tightly, and turn the bottle on its side or upside down. Observe.

Set the bottle upright, and unscrew the cap. Drop in half of the fizzy tablet and
enjoy the show!

2 KEEP THE SHOW GOING.

Turn the lights off, and shine a flashlight through the bottom of the bottle to
make your lava lamp look even groovier.

Drop in more fizzy tablets to make the reaction last longer.

CHEW ON THIS!

Oil and water don't mix. Because the oil is less dense than the water, it floats on top of it. The food coloring falls through the oil and mixes with the water. When you add the fizzy tablet, it sinks to the bottom and releases bubbles of carbon dioxide gas. Carbon dioxide is less dense than the oil and the water, so it rises to the surface. The gas takes drops of the colored water with it as it floats to the top. When the bubbles reach the top and pop, the gas escapes and the colored blobs sink back to the bottom.

DIG DEEPER

BLOB SCENE

Put the cap on the bottle and shake it up. What happens?

GET GROOVIER

Make more lava lamps—with a change or two. Does the temperature of the water make a difference? How about the size of the bottle or tablet piece? Does the experiment still work if the cap is off the bottle?

UNDER PRESSURE

Try supporting a book using just one sheet of paper.

> Unlike me, paper doesn't need to go to the gym to get stronger. All you need to do is change its shape.

What You'll Need:

• a few sheets of paper • a heavy book (such as a phone book or textbook)
• a ruler • scissors • tape

What to Do:

1 BRAINSTORM SOME IDEAS.

How might you use one sheet of paper so that it supports a book at least two inches above a tabletop for ten seconds? You can cut it, roll it into tubes, or fold, bend, twist, rip, crinkle, or crumple your paper!

2 MAKE YOUR SUPPORTS.

Choose one of your ideas. Follow your plan and use one sheet of paper to build a set of supports.

3 TEST AND REDESIGN.

Place the book on top of your supports. Count to ten. Did the paper support the book? It didn't? Get a new sheet of paper, and try, try again! It did? Congratulations, but don't stop. Keep going with the Dig Deeper challenges on the next page.

CHEW ON THIS!

Paper is thin and weak. Or is it? You can stiffen paper by changing its shape, like folding or rolling it into a column. But to support the most weight, you have to do one more thing. You have to turn the column so it's perpendicular to the pressure. Why? The more material (in this case, paper) you can move toward the column's ends and away from its middle, the more rigid the column becomes. As long as the column stays rigid, it continues to resist the pressure.

DIG DEEPER

DOUBLE DUTY

Using only one sheet of paper, support a book four inches above a table for at least ten seconds. Keep adding books until your supports collapse. Use a scale to weigh the books. Try to build a better support system to hold up this heavy stack of books.

PAPER BRIDGE CHALLENGE

Can you support a load of pennies using one sheet of paper? Put two equal-size stacks of books six inches apart. Make a bridge by placing a sheet of paper across the books. Put some pennies on the bridge. How many pennies can it support before it collapses? Can you change the design of your bridge to support more pennies?

COOL STUFF TO IMPRESS CHARLENE

Charlene is the poodle who lives next door. And no, I don't have a crush on her. She just happens to be the most incredible dog in the history of dogs. Or at least poodles. I haven't had the easiest time getting her to fall under the spell of the Ruffman. The poodle who has stolen my heart has acted a little cold to me lately. And by "lately," I mean ever since I met her. Maybe these projects will impress her enough to go on a date with me one day.

TARGET PRACTICE

Build a catapult using a lever, and power it with a rubber band. Then use what you've learned to build your own design, and send a marshmallow flying through the air!

I wrote my sweet Charlene a love note and need a way to deliver it to her backyard. I know! A catapult!

What You'll Need:

• toilet-paper or paper-towel tubes • cardboard boxes (such as shoe boxes, tissue boxes, cereal boxes, or milk cartons) • duct tape • plastic spoons • craft sticks • a pen • brass fasteners • rubber bands • mini marshmallows • a target (optional)

What to Do:

1 CONSTRUCT A CATAPULT.

Tape a toilet-paper tube to one of your cardboard boxes. This is your fulcrum.

Tape the handle of a plastic spoon to the end of a craft stick. This is your lever.

Use the pen to make a hole in the top of the tube, and insert the lever. Secure it with tape.

Use the pen to make a hole in the box in front of the tube, and attach a brass fastener.

Wrap a rubber band around the brass fastener, then around the middle of the lever (so that there is tension as you pull it back). Tape the rubber band in place.

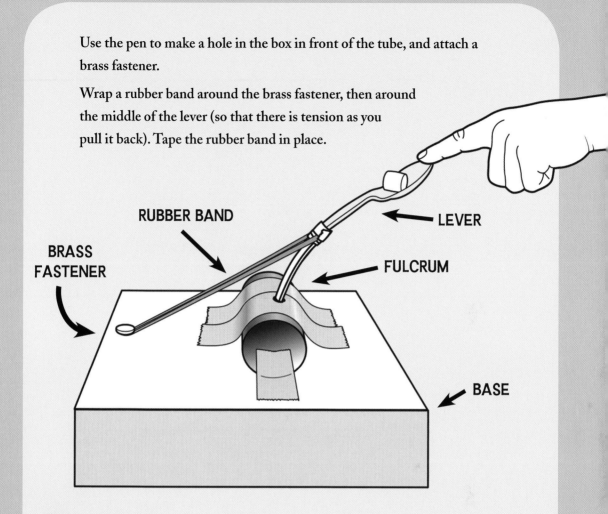

RUBBER BAND

BRASS FASTENER

LEVER

FULCRUM

BASE

2 LAUNCH IT!

Pull back on the lever, and put a marshmallow on the spoon. Then let go! What happens?

3 DESIGN YOUR OWN.

Now that you know how to build one kind of catapult, brainstorm your own design. Try a different base or fulcrum, build a different type of lever, or use the rubber band in a different way.

4 TEST AND REDESIGN.

Can your marshmallow hit a target? How can you make it go farther? Or higher? Change one thing (called a variable), like the length of the rubber band or the position of the lever. Predict what will happen. Test it!

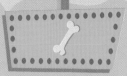

MINT LIGHTNING

Shoot lightning sparks from your mouth!

My dog breath will be minty fresh. Just in time to ask Charlene out on a date. Paws crossed that sparks will fly!

What You'll Need:

• a completely dark place (like a closet at night) • a fresh package of hard wintergreen mints made with wintergreen oil (not sugar-free) • a mirror
• a friend (optional)

What to Do:

1 GO DARK.

Go to your designated dark space, turn off the lights, and shut the door. Wait a few minutes for your eyes to adjust to the darkness.

2 CHOMP!

Pop a mint candy into your mouth. Then hold out the mirror (or ask a friend to watch you instead).

With your lips apart, chomp down hard on the candy to make a clean break.

3 OBSERVE AND EXPERIMENT.

What did you see when the candy broke? Try step 2 again to see if you can intensify the results.

CHEW ON THIS!

The spark you created in your mouth was actually a tiny version of lightning! Lightning is a powerful burst of electricity. In a thundercloud, small bits of ice rub against one another, creating an electrical charge. The charge of static electricity grows bigger and bigger, until—BOOM!—you see a giant bolt of lightning.

A similar reaction happens when you bite into the candy. As you crush the sugar crystals, the sugars release small electrical charges into the atmosphere, which attract the oppositely charged nitrogen in the air. This collision releases energy, which you see as tiny sparks of light.

But you can't make sparks with plain sugar. The oil of wintergreen is the chemical methyl salicylate, which absorbs ultraviolet light and transforms it into visible blue-green light. This process is called fluorescence.

3 Nitrogen molecules in the air have empty slots that attract the escaping electrons from the sugar. Once they combine, energy in the form of light is created.

Because the methyl salicylate (wintergreen oil) is present, the reaction glows!

1 The sugar molecules smash together when you bite them.

2 Crushing them forces a release of their negatively charged electrons into the atmosphere, where they are attracted to the oppositely charged nitrogen in the air.

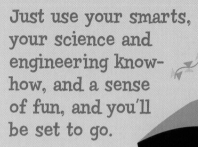

GO FLY A KITE

Just use your smarts, your science and engineering know-how, and a sense of fun, and you'll be set to go.

What You'll Need:

• a sheet of 8½" x 11" copier paper • a ruler • a pencil • tape • a wooden skewer • paper or fabric strips • a hole punch • a 3-foot-long piece of string

What to Do:

1 BUILD YOUR KITE.

Fold the paper in half.

On each side of the paper, draw two dots:
one 3 inches in from the fold (point A)
and the second 1 inch in from the fold (point B).
Draw a line connecting points A and B.

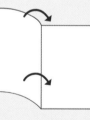
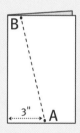

Fold the paper on these lines
to make the wings.

Put tape over the center line. Tape on the wooden skewer and a tail made of paper or a fabric strip.

Flip the kite so it rests on its top.

Fold the flap back and forth a couple of times until it stands straight up from the wings.

Punch a hole in the flap three inches from the smallest end of the flap.

Tie one end of the string to the hole. You're ready to fly!

2 FLY YOUR KITE.

Here are some tips for flying your kite:

Your body can block the air that the kite needs to fly properly. Keep the kite away from your body by holding it with your arm straight out to the side.

Hold the string lightly where it attaches to the kite. Let it out gradually when the kite tugs as it begins to fly.

CHEW ON THIS!

How do kites stay in the air? Remember, air isn't nothing—it's made of gas particles, such as oxygen, carbon dioxide, and nitrogen. As kites move through the air, the air pushes on the kite. But to keep a kite up, the air has to keep moving. Think of a water-skier. If the boat pulling a water-skier stops, the water-skier sinks. So for the kite to stay up, either you need to pull the kite through the air or the wind needs to blow against the kite. To keep a kite from falling, the upward force of the air hitting it must equal gravity's downward pull.

SET IT STRAIGHT

What do you get when you put a toilet-paper tube and a ruler together? A tabletop seesaw. Can you teach it some new tricks?

What You'll Need:

• tape • a toilet-paper tube • a ruler, paint stirrer, large craft stick, or yardstick
• small weights such as pennies or metal washers

What to Do:

1 BUILD YOUR SEESAW.

Tape the toilet-paper tube to the table as shown.

Note:

It's OK to have the platform touch the table while you're working on a challenge. It's also OK to move the platform and change where it touches the fulcrum. The weights don't have to be stacked or placed together on the platform.

This is your fulcrum, the point where your platform rests. Balance your ruler, stirrer, craft stick, or yardstick on top. This is your seesaw platform. Adjust the platform until it can balance parallel to the tabletop.

TRY THESE CHALLENGES.

The goal of each challenge is to have the platform be level, sitting parallel to the tabletop. Once it's level, it's balancing.

Put three weights on each end of the platform.

Put three weights on one side of the platform and six weights on the other.

Set the platform so one end sticks out twice as far beyond the fulcrum as the other end. Add weights until the platform is level.

Put ten weights on one end of the platform and none on the other end.

CHEW ON THIS!

With balancing, it's not just weight that matters. Position matters, too. Two things help keep your seesaw balanced: weight and distance. Weight is how much weight there is on each side of the fulcrum. Distance is how far each weight is from the fulcrum. Together, weight and distance create leverage. That's why, with your seesaw, you can balance a stack of pennies close to the fulcrum on one side with just one penny far from the fulcrum on the other side. Even though the single penny has only a little weight, it's far from the fulcrum, giving it a large amount of leverage.

DIG DEEPER

MAKE A MULTI-PLATFORM SEESAW

See what kind of wacky balance systems you can make by adjusting the positions of the platforms and the number of weights.

MAKE A MOBILE

Use pencils, string, and small objects to make a mobile. Adjust the positions of the strings and the objects strung on them so that the pencils hang parallel to the floor.

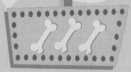

SIZE IT UP

Turn a small picture of Ruff into a large one. See how perfect the big picture has to be to still look like Ruff. Can we really trust our eyes?

I want to give Charlene a big picture of me, the very handsome Ruff Ruffman, for her living room. But the only photo I have is this tiny one. Help me enlarge my picture!

What You'll Need:

• pencils • a yardstick • chart paper or newspaper • 25 3-inch square sticky notes
• friends to help (optional)

What to Do:

1 MAKE A GRID.

Use the yardstick to draw a grid of 25 three-inch squares on the newspaper or chart paper. Label the columns 1–5 and the rows A–E.

2 CHOOSE SQUARES TO DRAW.

Look at the picture of Ruff. Using the row letters and column numbers (for example, A6), assign squares to yourself and to your friends.

3 ENLARGE THE SQUARE.

Copy everything in your square so it fills the entire sticky note. Find where the parts of the picture would be on your sticky note. For example, a line halfway up the right side of your square will also start halfway up the right side of the sticky note. Use your pencil to capture the white, gray, and black tones found in your square.

4 POST YOUR DRAWING.
Put the sticky note in the correct place on the grid. Repeat steps 3–4 with the other squares until the picture is complete.

5 EXAMINE THE PICTURE.
When the large picture is complete (or nearly complete), stand close to it. Note any lines, shading, or parts that don't line up perfectly. Then step back a few steps. Do the flaws stand out now? Finally, move to the other side of the room. Are you still aware of the flaws? What happened to them?

CHEW ON THIS!

From far away, the picture looks pretty good. But up close, you can see all sorts of flaws. Every moment, your brain collects an amazing amount of information. It then simplifies things for you by organizing the information into patterns. So parts of the picture may not be perfect, but from far away, your brain makes the pieces come together as a pattern that you recognize as Ruff. The eye and brain work together, like a team, to make sense of what you are seeing.

DIG DEEPER

EXTRA, EXTRA!

Look at a newspaper picture through a magnifying glass. Do you see a lot of dots? How far away do you have to hold the picture before the dots blend together and form the image?

GET TO THE POINT

Some painters use dabs of paint to create an image. As you move back from a painting, these dabs come together to form the image. Make a painting or drawing using different-colored dots.

OK, you made your point!

WHAT TO MAKE WHEN
I'M OUT OF CHINESE FOOD

Your parents always say, "Don't play with your food!" But where's the fun in that? I say, go ahead and play! My favorite food is Chinese food. But when I've licked the very last bit of *mu shu* from the takeout container, I sometimes whip up my own concoctions. Like Ruff's liver-and-pineapple biscuit shake! What? You don't dig meat-and-fruit smoothies? Fine. Then how about some candy and ice cream? Herring optional.

CANDY CRYSTALS

See how crystals form while making rock candy.

SAFETY TIPS

- Ask an adult for help!
- Don't touch the stove.

What You'll Need:

- a saucepan • ½ cup water • 1 cup sugar • a spoon • an oven mitt • a measuring cup
- a glass jar • cotton string • a pencil or wooden skewer • scissors • food coloring (optional)

What to Do:

1 DISSOLVE THE SUGAR IN WATER.

With the help of an adult, pour the water in a saucepan and bring it to a boil.

Add the sugar, one spoonful at a time, stirring constantly, until the sugar is dissolved into a clear syrup.

Let the solution cool for ten minutes, then pour it into the jar.

If you'd like, you can add a drop of food coloring.

2 CREATE YOUR CRYSTAL MAKER.

Tie one end of the string around the pencil or skewer.

Rest the pencil on top of the jar so the string hangs in the syrup without touching the jar's sides or bottom. Adjust the length of the string if necessary.

OBSERVE.

Check your crystal maker daily for a week. Draw a picture of what you see in your lab notebook. What is happening to the syrup?

CHEW ON THIS!

After three to seven days, the syrup should have turned into ready-to-eat candy crystals. You've just made rock candy! How? Heating the water forced more sugar to dissolve than would be possible at room temperature, causing supersaturation. The water could only hang onto the sugar if both stayed very hot. But when the supersaturated solution cooled, the water could no longer hold the extra sugar, so the sugar came out of the solution as sugar crystals. As time goes on and more water evaporates from the remaining solution, the solution becomes more saturated, and even more crystals form. Mmm, tasty!

Science Fair Tip

You could create a project that compares sugar crystals and salt crystals. Which ones grow faster? Why? Photograph each jar's contents every day and display them with your findings.

HOLD THE MOLD

Turn sandwich bread into a science experiment,
and find out where mold grows best.

I'd like to make a tasty sardine sandwich,
but my bread is looking a little green.
Ewwww.   What happened?

SAFETY TIP

- When you're done with this
  experiment, throw away
  ALL of the bags. Do not open
  the bags, inhale the mold spores,
  or eat the bread.

What You'll Need:

- cotton swabs • 5 slices of freshly baked (homemade or from a bakery) bread • salt
- 5 zippable plastic bags • a marker • a small cloth • water • a shoe box with a lid • tape
- a magnifying glass

What to Do:

1 PREPARE A DATA TABLE.

Include five columns (one for each sample) and fourteen rows (one for each day
you'll observe the mold's growth).

2 COLLECT SOME MOLD SPORES.

Run the cotton swabs over a dusty area of your house, such as under a bed.
Rub a dusty swab over each slice of bread.

3 PREPARE YOUR BREAD.

Sample 1: Sprinkle salt on one of the bread slices. Seal it in a plastic bag labeled SALT.

Sample 2: Seal the next slice with a small wet cloth in a bag labeled HUMID.

Sample 3: Seal this slice in a bag labeled NO LIGHT. Put the first three samples
in a shoe box.

Sample 4: Seal this slice in a bag labeled WITH LIGHT. Leave it in a sunny place indoors.

Sample 5: Seal the last slice in a bag labeled COLD and stick it in the refrigerator.

 4 **MAKE A PREDICTION.**
Which slices of bread do you think will grow the most mold? The least? Record your predictions in your lab notebook.

5 **OBSERVE, RECORD, AND DRAW CONCLUSIONS.**
Examine the pieces of bread <u>at a fixed time</u> every day for two weeks. Note the bread's color, amount of mold coverage, and texture.

Look at the mold under the magnifying glass. Which conditions help mold grow the fastest? Why? Write down your observations in your lab notebook.

CHEW ON THIS!

Those fuzzy green-gray spots on your bread and other food that's been hanging around too long is called mold, a microscopic, living organism. Mold is a fungus, which means it's related to yeast and mushrooms. Its spores are present everywhere; that's why you were able to collect them from the dust in your house.

Mold thrives in places that are warm, dark, and moist. So the bread kept in one or more of those conditions — samples 2, 3, and 4 — grows moldy the fastest. The slice you put in the fridge, sample 5, experiences a slower growth because of the fridge's cold temperature. The slice with salt, sample 1, also has less mold because salt is a natural preservative.

DIG DEEPER

BAKERY LAB
Try growing mold on various types of breads, kept at the same temperature. Is mold growth affected by the type of bread?

SHADES OF MOLD
See if you can grow mold on cheese or soft fruit, like lemons and strawberries. Does mold look different on different types of food?

Science Fair Tip

Take videos or pictures of the mold every day. Chart the growth of the mold for each slice.

ICE-CREAM SHAKE

OK, let's shake things up and turn a liquid into a solid. If you succeed, you'll have a tasty treat to enjoy at the end. Yum!

What You'll Need:

• ½ cup cream • 1 tablespoon sugar • 1 teaspoon vanilla • a quart-size zippable plastic bag • a gallon-size zippable plastic bag • 2 cups ice • ¼ cup salt • paper towels • cups or bowls and spoons (for tasting)

What to Do:

1 MIX THE INGREDIENTS.

Put the cream, sugar, and vanilla into the small bag. Squeeze out any extra air, and zip the bag closed. Check it twice to make sure it's completely sealed.

2 ADD ICE.

Put the small bag into the big bag. Add the ice and salt to the big bag. Then seal the big bag tightly.

3 SHAKE THE MIXTURE.

Gently shake the bags for about 10 minutes or until the cream feels solid. What changes do you notice in the cream as you shake? What is happening to the ice and salt mixture?

TASTE THE RESULTS.

When the cream feels solid, remove the small bag. Dry the outside of it with paper towels so the salty water doesn't get in your ice cream. Cut the corner off your bag. Squeeze the ice cream into cups or bowls. Enjoy!

Heat energy flows from the cream to the ice, cooling the cream and melting the ice.

CHEW ON THIS!

Cold doesn't exist by itself. Cold just means there's less heat energy around. Take a cold room, for example. It's cold because it doesn't contain a lot of heat energy. Some of its heat energy escaped! To make ice cream, you must remove heat energy from the cream. That's why you use ice. Heat energy moves from places with more heat energy to places with less. So heat energy flows from the cream to the ice, cooling the cream and melting the ice. Once the cream loses enough heat energy, it freezes and becomes a solid. Once the ice gains enough heat energy, it melts and becomes a liquid.

DIG DEEPER

WHICH WAY?

Find examples of freezing and melting. Look for things like food freezing or thawing or ice forming or melting. Decide which direction the heat energy is moving.

CREAMY?

Put half a cup of the cream mixture into the freezer. Don't shake it. When it's frozen, how does its texture compare to the ice cream you made in the bag?

PASS THE SALT

Fill two cups with ice and water. Take the temperature with a thermometer. Is it the same? Add two tablespoons of salt to one of the cups and mix. After five minutes, measure the temperature in both cups again. Is it the same? If not, which is colder?

ALMOST AS FUN AS SQUEAKY TOYS

Being a celebrity, I once asked Blossom to create a Ruff
action figure we could sell to stores everywhere. I imagined
that Action Ruff could do ultra-hip, ultra-fun actions, like
karate, funky dance moves, flips, barracuda-fast swimming,
and strutting. Blossom, however, thought it would be more
accurate if Action Ruff's sole action was "being blobby." Not
exactly what I had in mind. Maybe you can do better with
these toys. . . .

MOTION PICTURE

Create a thaumatrope — an optical-illusion toy that makes two pictures look like one.

What You'll Need:

• 3" x 5" index cards • markers or crayons • tape • a hole punch or pencil • rubber bands • a friend

What to Do:

1 MAKE A THAUMATROPE.

Draw a cage in the middle of an index card.

Draw a bird in the middle of a second index card.

Tape the cards together with the images facing out.

Punch a hole on each side of the attached index cards.

Loop a rubber band through each hole so that they're securely tied to the cards.

2 WIND IT UP AND LET IT GO!

Hold on to each rubber band and have a partner turn the thaumatrope around and around, winding up the rubber bands until they are tight.

Then have your partner let go. What do you see? Are both images right side up?

If necessary, rearrange the cards so that each image appears right side up as it spins.

3 EXPERIMENT.

Try drawing different pictures such as a fish and fishbowl, flowers and a vase, a sailboat and the ocean, a surfer and wave, or come up with your own! What kinds of pictures work best?

Make a thaumatrope with words instead of pictures (like "GO" and "FETCH!"). Can you make it work?

CHEW ON THIS!

When the thaumatrope spins, the two pictures move so fast that your brain holds on to each image for a fraction of a second, and you see both together at the same time! This is called the persistence of vision.

The more tightly you wind up the rubber bands, the faster and longer your thaumatrope spins! By winding up the rubber bands, you're storing energy (called potential energy). When you let go of the rubber bands, energy is released and turned into the energy of motion (kinetic energy), and the thaumatrope spins.

DIG DEEPER

FLIP IT

A flip book also creates the illusion of movement. Get a small pad of paper and a pen. On the last page, draw a simple picture, such as a stick figure or ball. To make the picture look like it's moving, draw the same thing on the next sheet from the bottom, but place it in a slightly different position. Do this for five to ten more pages. Then flip the pages forward and backward for your own mini-movie!

Flip the pages to create your own mini-movie!

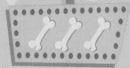

MYSTERY SAND

Can sand stay dry in water? Solve the mystery by following the clues in this intriguing experiment.

SAFETY TIPS

- Ask an adult for help!
- Do not inhale the spray.

What You'll Need:

- a large box lid • a measuring cup • 2 cups of clean sand (found at a crafts store)
- silicone spray lubricant (found at a hardware store) • 2 small clear plastic cups
- water • a spoon • a zippable plastic bag (optional)

What to Do:

1 WHIP UP SOME MYSTERY SAND.

Make the mystery sand outside. Spread one cup of the clean sand in the box lid, and spray it with the silicone.

Shake the sand around and spray it again. Repeat three times.

Let it dry overnight.

2 TEST YOUR MYSTERY SAND.

Fill one of the cups ¾ full with water.

Sprinkle your mystery sand until the water's surface is coated.

Gently push your finger into the layer of sand and toward the bottom of the cup.

Remove your finger. What happens?

CHEW ON THIS!

Did you solve the mystery behind the mystery sand? Let's crack the case! When ordinary sand is poured into water, it becomes wet and clumpy. However, your mystery sand is coated with silicone, a special substance that's hydrophobic, or "water-fearing," meaning it repels water molecules. Untreated sand, however, is hydrophilic, or "water-loving," so the water molecules are attracted to it.

When you dip your finger into the water, the layer of mystery sand on the water's surface becomes a barrier between your finger and the water. Gently pushing down on the water stretches the water's surface, but as long as you don't poke through it, the mystery sand keeps your finger dry. Case closed!

DIG DEEPER

MIX IT UP

In two clean cups of water, stir in a spoonful of each of the sands. What happens to the mystery sand? What happens to the untreated sand?

JUST A SPOONFUL

Bring up some of each type of sand with a spoon, and touch them. Do you feel a difference?

Science Fair Tip

You can do this experiment at the fair. (To reuse the mystery sand, pour it on paper towels to dry and then store it in a zippable plastic bag.) Ask people to compare the sands by putting them in water and taking them out.

KALEID-O-MANIA

Reflections, light, and your artistic talents create a dazzling kaleidoscope!

Oooh . . . I wish I could see more than limited colors!

What You'll Need:

• 8" x 11" transparency film (for overhead projectors) • a ruler • a sharpened pencil
• scissors • clear tape • a paper-towel tube • a small 3-ounce paper cup (unwaxed)
• colored markers

What to Do:

1 MAKE A KALEIDOSCOPE.

Cut the transparency film into 1¼-inch by 11-inch strips.

Tape the long edges of the three strips of the transparency film together, forming a triangular cylinder. Line up the edges of the strips carefully, and use as little tape as possible.

Slide the cylinder into the paper-towel tube. Look through it. What do you see?

Using markers, draw a colorful design on the inside bottom of the cup.

Place the cup over one end of the tube and look through the other side. Turn the cup.

What do you see—and where do you see it? At the front of the tube? On the sides?

PREDICT, EXPERIMENT, AND OBSERVE.

Predict what will happen if you change one thing (called a variable) on your kaleidoscope. What would happen if you change:

- the design on the cup?
- the reflecting surfaces inside? (What if you use a rolled-up piece of transparency film instead of a triangle?)
- how light enters the tube? (What if you cover the cup with your hand or poke a few small holes into the bottom of the cup?)

Try it, and see if your prediction was right!

CHEW ON THIS!

Kaleidoscopes use reflecting surfaces (like mirrors or shiny smooth plastic) to produce beautiful patterns. Reflections of your design are mirrored in the shiny surfaces of the transparency film. Those reflections bounce back and forth off the three sides, creating even more reflections. When you rotate the cup, the reflected designs shift and change. All this depends on light—put your hand over the cup and block all the light, and you'll see nothing!

DIG DEEPER

HALL OF MIRRORS
Place two small mirrors in a V shape on top of a magazine or picture. Change the angle of the mirrors by moving them closer together or farther apart. What happens?

MIRROR WRITING
Write your name on a piece of paper and hold it up to a mirror. What do you notice? Keep holding the paper up to the mirror, and on a different sheet, copy the letters exactly as you see them. Then hold that paper up to the mirror. What do you see now?

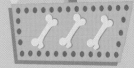

THRILL RIDE

Design a crazy roller-coaster ride
for a marble — but make sure it
doesn't fly off the track!

I'm throwing Chet a birthday party.
Help me build a pint-size roller coaster
to give the little guy a big thrill!

What You'll Need:

• 6-foot foam pipe insulation tubing, ¾ inch or 1 inch in diameter • scissors
• masking tape • various props: boxes, books, chairs, buckets, cups • marbles
• toilet-paper tubes (optional)

What to Do:

1 MAKE TRACKS.

Cut your foam pipe insulation tubing in half lengthwise.
Start your track at the top of a high place: tape one end of the
tubing to the top of a ledge, table, or other high spot.

2 CHALLENGE YOURSELF.

Use props (like chairs, books, and boxes) to design different kinds
of roller-coaster courses. Steady your track with tape where needed.
Use toilet-paper rolls as tunnels. Try:

♦ two hills

♦ a hill and a sharp turn

♦ a loop-de-loop — the ultimate challenge!

TEST AND REDESIGN.

Send your marble on a wild ride and see what happens! If your marble jumps the track or runs out of energy before the end, it's time to redesign. Are your hills too steep, or not steep enough? Is your track steady or wobbly? Test out different solutions until your coaster is as cool as you want it to be.

CHEW ON THIS!

Did you notice that your starting point has to be the highest point on the course? The higher the starting point, the more potential energy your marble has stored up to use later. When the marble starts rolling downward, its potential energy begins to change into kinetic energy (the energy of motion). If it has enough energy, your marble will make it up the next hill or even around the loop-de-loop!

DIG DEEPER

FREESTYLE

Find a partner and combine your tracks to double the fun. How many turns, loops, and hills can you have and still make sure the marble reaches the end of the course?

SKI JUMP

Construct a ski jump with the roller-coaster track and some props, and watch your marble take flight! How far can it go?

TOY CHEMISTRY

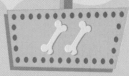

Mix two liquids together to form a gooey solid that you can mold and stretch into weird shapes. This is chemistry at its craziest!

SAFETY TIPS

- Ask an adult for help!
- Keep mixtures away from clothes, eyes, and mouth.
- Goo should not touch fabric or paper, only hard surfaces, since it sticks to things easily.

What You'll Need:

- 2 clear plastic cups • measuring spoons • water • 2 teaspoons white glue • food coloring
- ¼ teaspoon borax • plastic spoons • a plastic knife • a zippable plastic bag for storage

What to Do:

1 MIX THE INGREDIENTS.

In a cup, mix two teaspoons of water with the white glue. Then add two drops of food coloring. In another cup, mix two teaspoons of water with the borax.

H₂O

BORAX

2 COMBINE THE MIXTURES.

Pour the borax mixture into the glue mixture, and stir. When the two are mixed, what happens? Take the goo into your hands, and play with it.

3 EXPERIMENT AND MAKE OBSERVATIONS.

Does your slimy goo act more like a liquid or a solid—or a little like both? Find out all the things it can do: try to stretch it, bounce it, flatten it, twist it, roll it, jiggle it, rip it apart, or use your knife to cut it into shapes. Does it keep its shape if you leave it alone for a while?

WHAT CAN THE GOO DO?

ACTION	OBSERVATION
STRETCH	
BOUNCE	
FLATTEN	
TWIST	
ROLL	
JIGGLE	
RIP	
CUT	
LEAVE ALONE	

CHEW ON THIS!

You just created a polymer. Many polymers are flexible plastics, like balloons, plastic water bottles, and the soles of your sneakers. Some polymers, like those used on back tricycle wheels, are strong and hard, yet flexible enough to absorb shocks and allow for a smooth ride. Other polymers, like chewing gum or the slimy goo you just made (which contains mostly water), are soft and stretchy.

How did you make a polymer? Combining the borax and glue mixtures causes a chemical reaction. By themselves, glue molecules move about freely (until they dry). But when you add borax, it binds the slippery glue molecules together in a web, so they can't move around as much. Borax turns the watery glue into a denser, more rubbery substance.

Glue Molecule

The stretchy bond created by chemical reaction binds the two molecules together and creates a rubbery substance.

Borax Molecule

Glue Molecule

WHO'S A GOOD HUMAN?

Every day, FETCHers like you show me how intelligent, inventive, and amazing humans really are. Plus you have hands. HANDS! Do you know how many dogs wish *they* could open the refrigerator door? But let's face it, even humans aren't perfect. Try out the next set of challenges, and see what I mean. Test your senses, balance, brains, and burping abilities!

EXCUSE YOU!

Here's your chance to create burps and other rude noises in the name of science!

What You'll Need:

• a small plastic bottle • vinegar • a funnel • baking soda • a balloon (stretched out to make it flexible)

What to Do:

1 GET READY TO BURP.

Fill $1/3$ of the bottle with vinegar.

Using the funnel, fill half of the deflated balloon with baking soda.

Pull the mouth of the balloon over the neck of the bottle, and let the balloon fall to the side to keep the baking soda from getting into the bottle.

Raising one end of the balloon, drop the baking soda into the bottle all at once. The balloon will inflate.

2 LET 'ER RIP!

Once your balloon has inflated, you're ready to make burps.

Carefully release the balloon from the bottle and listen.

CHEW ON THIS!

A burp is simply the escape of air from your belly. When you eat or drink, you swallow air at the same time. The trapped air (gases such as nitrogen and oxygen) builds up in the stomach and needs to leave. So it's forced up your esophagus and out of your mouth as a . . . BURP! You also burp after drinking carbonated drinks such as soda, which are loaded with carbon dioxide bubbles.

Carbon dioxide is the same gas that filled your balloon. In this experiment, you make carbon dioxide when you mix an acid (vinegar) with a base (baking soda). The result? Lots of rude noises!

DIG DEEPER

GO BIG

Can you make a larger balloon by adding more vinegar or baking soda?

RISING ACTION

Mix two teaspoons of yeast with a cup of warm water. Add one teaspoon of sugar and pour the mixture into a small plastic bottle. Stretch the balloon over the bottle neck, and set it aside for an hour. What happens?

THAT'S ONE BIG BALLOON!

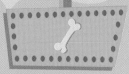

SMELL YOU LATER!

Can you still taste food when you plug your nose?

Hello? Chet . . . you have a phone? Why yes, I am eating smelly cheese. . . .

SAFETY TIP

- Ask an adult for help cutting the fruits and vegetables with the knife, as it's sharp!

What You'll Need:

• 4 opaque cups • milk • water • orange juice • soda • masking tape • a marker
• a blindfold • a friend • a potato • an apple • an onion • a knife

What to Do:

1 GET YOUR DRINKS READY.

Pour one of the four liquids into each cup. Using the masking tape and marker, label what's in each one.

Put on the blindfold. Then ask your friend to rearrange the cups so you don't know the order of the drinks.

2 DRINK UP!

Your friend should now pass you one drink at a time. Take a sip of each. Can you identify each drink?

Try the drinks again in another order, and this time hold your nose. Can you still guess which drink is which?

3 TAKE A BITE.

Repeat the experiment using solid food. Ask a friend to place one equal-size piece of potato, apple, and onion on your tongue one at a time. Rinse your mouth with water between each bite. Can you guess what you're eating based only on how it tastes? Next, try it while holding your nose.

CHEW ON THIS!

Did you know that most of what we taste is actually what we smell? That's because your nose and mouth are connected through the same airway, so you smell and taste at the same time. Holding your nose while tasting the drinks and food makes it difficult to taste the difference between them. But when you unplug your nose, you should have been able to taste all of the flavors again. (Sorry about the onion breath!)

DIG DEEPER

SWEET, SOUR, BITTER, SALTY

Test your taste buds. Fill four cups, each with a different liquid — soda, lemon juice, tonic water, and salty water. Dip a cotton swab in the soda, and dab it on each area of your tongue. Does it taste stronger in one area than another? Rinse your mouth and repeat for the other drinks.

THE GREAT JELLY BEAN TEST

Does the sense of sight affect taste? Find out with this taste test. Get two each of cherry, lime, lemon, and orange jelly beans. Ask a friend to taste one of each with eyes open and guess the flavors. Then ask your friend to repeat the experiment with eyes closed. How many flavors did he or she guess correctly?

Science Fair Tip

Try this taste test on your friends. Make a graph showing the correct guesses for each of the drinks without the nose blocked, and another for the correct guesses with the nose blocked.

THROW YOUR WEIGHT AROUND

Fortunately, we don't usually have to think about keeping our balance. But how do we stay balanced? It's trickier than you think. Challenge yourself with these three moves!

What You'll Need:

• Just yourself!

What to Do:

 1 THE HEAVY FOOT.

Your foot doesn't weigh very much, does it? Well, try this:

Stand sideways next to a wall, with your right side against it.

Put your right shoulder, right cheek, and side of your right foot directly against the wall.

Lift your left foot off the floor. What happens?

Now move six inches away from the wall and lift your left foot off the floor. How did your body shift to help you stay balanced? Why couldn't you move this way the first time?

2 GLUED TO THE WALL.

Picking something up is easy, right? Well, try this:

Stand with your back against a wall.

Place a small object, such as a coin or wad of paper, on the floor about 12 inches in front of your feet.

Put your feet together and your heels against the wall.

Try to pick up the object without moving your feet or bending your knees.

Now step away from the wall and pick up the object. How did your body shift to help you stay balanced? Why couldn't you move this way the first time?

3 THE SEAT THAT CAN'T BE BEAT.

How hard can it be to get out of a chair? Try this:

Sit on a straight-backed, armless chair. Make sure your feet can reach the floor.

Cross your arms over your chest.

Keep your feet flat on the floor and your back straight. Try to stand up.

Now get out of the chair the way you usually do. How did your body shift to help you stand up? What is your body doing so you can get out of the chair?

CHEW ON THIS!

When you are standing and lean forward or stick out an arm or a leg, do you realize that you always move another part of your body in the opposite direction to stay balanced? For example, when you lean forward, gravity pulls your head and shoulders toward the ground. To stay balanced, you move your hips back. With gravity pulling your hips toward the ground, the two pulls cancel each other out and you don't fall over.

Fortunately, your brain automatically moves your legs, feet, arms, head, and everything else to keep you stable. Dancers and athletes are exceptionally good at sensing how they have to move their bodies to stay balanced.

DIG DEEPER

TWO LEGS OR FOUR?
Do animals with four legs have better balance? Get on your hands and knees. In this position, how easy is it to lean way over to one side? What do you have to do to stay balanced?

TRUE TALENT
Figure skaters do triple lutzes, dancers leap and twirl, and gymnasts pull off back flips. Watch a performance and observe how people move their bodies to maintain their balance.

Challenge Points 10

TRAIN YOUR BRAIN

Can you train your brain to ignore something? This challenge — called a Stroop test — plays a little trick on you. But maybe you're too quick for the trick!

> My brain is amazing! I can identify 47 different smells from a hundred yards away with my eyes closed. Look – a squirrel outside! Oops, sorry – I got a little distracted. Maybe you can help me figure out how to stay focused.

What You'll Need:

• 2 blank 4 x 4 grids (to make a grid, copy the example shown) • crayons, pens, or markers — at least four different colors • a ruler • a stopwatch or clock • a friend

What to Do:

PART 1: THE WORDS MATCH THE COLORS.

1 FILL IN ONE GRID.

Choose a marker. Use it to write the name of its color in one of the grid boxes. For example, if you chose a red marker, you'd write the word RED in one of the boxes. Fill in the grid this way, using at least four different colors.

2 PLAY THE GAME.

Have one person be the timer and one be the reader. When the timer says, "Go," the reader reads the word in each box out loud. If he or she makes a mistake, he or she should read the word again correctly. On the chart on page 68, record how many seconds it takes the reader to read the sixteen words correctly.

66

3 PLAY AGAIN.

Switch roles. Repeat step 2.

PART 2: THE WORDS DON'T MATCH THE COLORS.

4 FILL IN THE OTHER GRID.

Now write the name of a color that's *different* from the ink color. So, if you chose a red marker, you'd write *BLUE, GREEN, YELLOW,* or some such in the box. Fill in the grid this way, using at least four different colors.

5 MAKE A PREDICTION.

How long will it take you to name the ink colors instead of reading the words? Write your prediction in a chart like the one on page 68.

6 PLAY AGAIN.

Play as in step 2. But this time, the reader says the *color of the ink* used in each box. For example, if the box contains the word BLUE written with a red marker, the reader should say "Red." Record how long it takes the reader to say all sixteen colors correctly. Switch roles and play again.

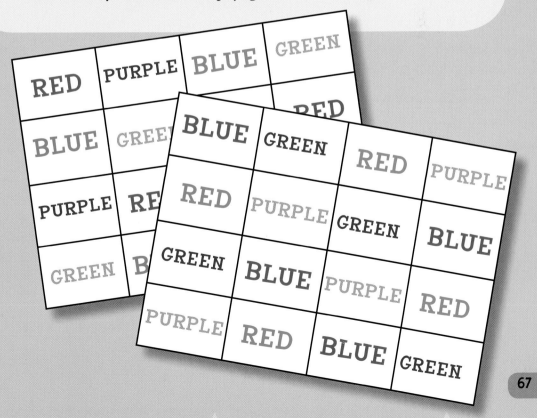

	Reader 1	Reader 2
Time in Part 1		
Prediction for Part 2		
Time in Part 2		

CHEW ON THIS!

In part 2, your brain gets two signals from your eyes—the words and the ink color. Reading is very automatic for most people. But naming a color isn't. To name the color, your mind has to ignore its first reaction—what a word says. But ignoring something can take real mental effort! In fact, when you do something that takes a lot of concentration, like a Stroop test, your brain can get tired. This makes it hard to stay focused. Want to do better? Scientists say giving yourself a break before trying again helps. Taking a quick walk outside is a good way to rest the parts of the brain you use for concentrating.

DIG DEEPER

STRATEGIES FOR SUCCESS
Does practice make perfect, or do you do better by giving yourself a relaxing break? Or does doing BOTH give the best results? See which approach improves your time the most.

TIME-SENSITIVE
Try testing at different times of the day, when people are more likely to be alert or tired.

UPSIDE DOWN
What if it's hard to read the words? Do part 2 again. But this time, turn the grid upside down and try testing again.

COLOR-FREE
Is it easier if the words aren't colors? Make a new grid using non-color words, such as BALL or CUP.

FOR SPY HOUNDS ONLY
(TOP-SECRET PROJECTS!)

Ruff Ruffman's Notes to Self—How to Be a Spy:

1. Wear a snazzy tuxedo or at least a bow tie.
2. Spend an hour in front of a mirror striking poses and saying in my best James Bond accent: "Ruffman. Ruff Ruffman."
3. Master these spy-related science experiments.
4. Don't tell ANYBODY how to do them!
5. Ummmm . . . you're reading this, aren't you?
6. New rule: Tell Secret Agent FETCHer (that's *you*!) to keep these projects hush-hush. I can trust you, right?

OPERATION ESPIONAGE

Your mission is to write with invisible ink and figure out the best way to reveal a secret message.

A notorious canine spy named Ken L. Koff is smuggling secret messages inside his dog collar! Blossom intercepted one, but it's written with invisible ink. Help!

Pretty Sneaky

What You'll Need:

• 1 teaspoon baking soda • water • a cup • a spoon • paper • cotton swabs • 3 bowls, filled halfway with purple grape juice, grape juice concentrate, and cranberry juice, each labeled • a bowl filled halfway with water, with a drop of red and blue food coloring, labeled COLORED WATER • cotton balls • a pencil • paper towels

What to Do:

1 MIX THE INGREDIENTS.

Combine the baking soda and one teaspoon of water in a cup and stir. You've just made invisible ink!

2 WRITE WITH INVISIBLE INK.

Fold a sheet of paper into four equal parts. Then unfold it.

Dip a cotton swab into the invisible ink mixture and use it like a pen to write a secret message on each of the four sections. Write something short (like your initials or "RUFF"), since there's not much room.

Let the paper dry completely, which takes about ten minutes. You may need to fan it in the air to help it along. What happens to your messages as they dry?

3 REVEAL THE SECRET MESSAGE!

While your paper dries, line up the bowls filled with different kinds of liquids.

On each section of paper, test a different liquid. Starting with one section, dip your cotton ball in one of the juices. Squeeze out the excess juice. Gently pat (don't rub) the cotton over one of the sections of paper.

Did your message appear?

Test each liquid on the three remaining sections of your paper. Use a new cotton ball each time. Does one liquid work better than the others to reveal the hidden message?

What color is the message?

CHEW ON THIS!

When you patted the juice on the dried baking soda, you caused a chemical reaction! Baking soda is what chemists call a base. The juices are acids. When a base and an acid come in contact, a chemical reaction can occur. Some chemical reactions result in a change in color, which is what happens here. The chemical reaction turns the invisible message bluish green, and that's why you can read it!

RUFF RULES!

EYE SPY

Make a periscope so you can secretly
peer over walls and peek around corners.

SAFETY TIP

- It's difficult to cut the
  carton with scissors.
  Ask an adult for help!

What You'll Need:

• a milk carton (quart size, thoroughly washed and dried) • scissors • 2 small rectangular
mirrors, approximately 2½" x 3½" (glass or plastic) • duct tape

What to Do:

1 CUT THE CARTON.

Ask an adult to cut off the top of the milk carton.

Cut out a square about ¼ inch from the bottom of the carton. This will be your
eyehole—make it large enough so you can see through it.

On the opposite side of the milk carton, about ¼ inch from the top, cut out a
larger square, at least twice the size of the eyehole.

2 ADD A MIRROR.

Place a mirror at the bottom of the milk carton. Position it as shown in the
diagram. Tape it in place.

Look through the eyehole. You should be able to see the ceiling of the room
you're in reflected in the mirror. If you don't, change the angle of the mirror.

3 ADD ANOTHER MIRROR.

Tape the top edge of the second mirror (facing down) to the top edge of the milk carton, on the side where you cut out the large square. Position the bottom edge as shown in the diagram, and tape it in place.

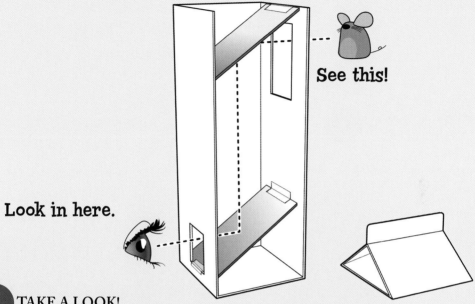

See this!

Look in here.

4 TAKE A LOOK!

EXPERIMENT. Can you look over a shelf? Around a corner? Under a table?

OBSERVE. While looking through the eyehole, put your hand on the carton where you think you're looking out. Did you find it right away? It's trickier than you think!

CHEW ON THIS!

You see things when light bounces off an object and reaches your eye. The mirrors in the periscope reflect light. They're angled so that the top mirror reflects the light down to the bottom mirror, and the bottom mirror reflects it into your eye. When you look through the eyehole and peer over a ledge, it seems like you're seeing something directly in front of you, at eye level. But you're actually seeing something several inches higher!

DIG DEEPER

SCOPE IT OUT

Use two milk cartons to make a taller periscope by taping the open ends of the cartons together. Or make a periscope out of an aluminum-foil or plastic-wrap box (have an adult remove the serrated edge). What can you do with a longer periscope?

WHODUNIT?

Detectives say Grandma Ruff baked a metal file into a cake to help Ruff's notorious brother Scruff break out of jail — and now she's been arrested! The cake included baking soda, and a similar-looking powder was found on Grandma Ruff's apron. The secret is in the science — if it's not baking soda, she's innocent!

SAFETY TIPS
- Ask an adult for help!
- Keep mixtures away from clothes, eyes, and mouth.
- No tasting!

Sweet old Grandma would never turn to a life of crime! Help clear her name!

What You'll Need:

• a friend • sticky notes (to use as labels) • a pencil • 3 cups, each with 1 teaspoon of baking powder • 3 cups, each with 1 teaspooon of flour • 3 cups, each with 1 teaspoon of baking soda • 3 cups, each with 1 teaspoon of the "mystery substance"* • purple grape juice • white vinegar • iodine • 3 pipettes or eyedroppers • paper towels

* Ask a friend to fill up the three cups of mystery substance WITHOUT revealing its identity. (Your partner can find out what the mystery substance is by reading "Chew on This!" on page 76. As for you, NO PEEKING!)

What to Do:

1 SET UP YOUR WORKSTATION.

Make labels for each powder and liquid listed on the illustration, and arrange them in a grid. Place the cups with baking powder, flour, and baking soda above their labels. (Your cups with the mystery substance come later!)

② TEST, OBSERVE, AND RECORD.

Using a pipette or eyedropper, put 5 to 10 drops of grape juice in the first cup of baking powder. What happens? Write your observations in your lab notebook. Now try the grape juice on the other two powders, recording your observations each time.

③ WHAT'S HAPPENING?

In some cases, a chemical reaction will occur. Signs of this include foaming, fizzing, or a change in color. But sometimes no chemical reaction can be seen. Can you tell the difference?

4 REPEAT STEPS 2 AND 3

Test all the liquids with all the powders and write down your observations. Use a new pipette with each liquid.

5 TEST THE MYSTERY SUBSTANCE!

Get 3 cups of the mystery substance and line them up next to the grape juice, vinegar, and iodine. Test and record your observations. (Hint: The mystery substance is one of the powders you already tested!)

6 COMPARE DATA AND DRAW CONCLUSIONS.

Did your observations about the mystery substance match any of the powders you tested? By comparing your data, can you figure out what the mystery substance is? Explain your reasons. Did you prove Grandma Ruffman's innocence?

CHEW ON THIS!

In this activity, you performed an experiment and analyzed data like a scientist does. As long as the conditions are the same, a chemical will react in the same way every time. You set up the experiment so that each powder was tested in exactly the same way. Then you observed the chemical reactions closely and recorded your data. When you drew conclusions about what the mystery substance was, your conclusions were supported by scientific evidence.

Did you prove Grandma Ruffman's innocence? The cake at the crime scene was made with baking soda, but the mystery substance on Grandma Ruffman's apron was . . .

baking powder!

BEYOND THE TOILET BOWL

It may surprise you to discover that water is good for more than just drinking out of the toilet. (Er, judging from your reaction, maybe that's only surprising to my dog friends.) ANYWAY, water is also a fascinating topic for science fair experiments. Get ready to make your own weather and do impossible stunts, like bending water and making eggs float! Don't believe me? Then read on, my fine FETCHer friend. . . .

RAINING CATS AND DOGS

How does acid rain affect plants?
Make your own weather and find out!

Sure, make rain.
Who doesn't love
the sweet perfume
of wet dog?

What You'll Need:

• 3 potted plants (all the same size and type) • 3 spray bottles • masking tape • a marker
• water • vinegar • a ruler

What to Do:

1 PREPARE A DATA TABLE.

Copy the one on page 80 into your lab notebook.

2 PREPARE THE PLANTS AND SPRAY BOTTLES.

Using the masking tape, label the plants and spray bottles:
REGULAR RAIN, ACID RAIN, and EXTREME ACID RAIN.

Fill the bottles with the following liquids:

REGULAR RAIN: water only

ACID RAIN: $2/3$ water and $1/3$ vinegar

EXTREME ACID RAIN: $1/3$ water and $2/3$ vinegar

Water each plant with the type of "rain" noted on its label. Give the same
amount to each plant.

Place the plants in the same location, where they'll all get the same amount of sunlight.

Record the heights and colors of the plants in your lab notebook.

WATER AND MEASURE THE PLANTS.

Over the next three weeks, water each plant with the type of rain that matches its label.

Every week, measure the heights and colors of the three plants and record their growth.

Observe the color of the plants' stems and leaves. Record these findings, too.

COMPARE THE PLANTS AND DRAW CONCLUSIONS.

After three weeks, observe how the different types of rain affected the plants. How do they compare to one another?

Science Fair Tip

Display photos of the plants at various stages of growth. Make sure to include your ruler in the pictures.

	WEEK 1		WEEK 2		WEEK 3	
	HEIGHT	COLOR	HEIGHT	COLOR	HEIGHT	COLOR
PLANT 1 REGULAR RAIN						
PLANT 2 ACID RAIN						
PLANT 3 EXTREME ACID RAIN						

80

CHEW ON THIS!

The plants that you water with acidic water grow more slowly than the one without. The plant that receives extremely acidic water grows the slowest and likely dies. That's because acid rain is bad news for plants, as well as a lot of other things on earth. It's caused by air pollution that begins with the burning of fossil fuels, such as oil and coal. When these fuels burn, they release sulfur dioxide and nitrogen oxide into the atmosphere, where they mix with water, oxygen, and other chemicals to form acid rain.

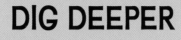

DIG DEEPER

RAIN MAKER

See how rain forms! With an adult's help, boil about three inches of water in a teakettle. Using an oven mitt, hold a metal pie plate full of ice about six inches above the kettle. What happens to the bottom of the pie plate?

SAFETY TIP

- Ask an adult for help to boil water on the stove.

THE INCREDIBLE FLOATING EGG

Eggs can't float. Or can they?
Try this eggs-periment to find out!

I don't know much about eggs, but I happen to be a world-renowned eggs-pert on egg rolls. Yum. Egg-roll experiment, anyone? C'mon. A N Y O N E ?

8

9

10

What You'll Need:

• 2 glasses • water • salt • 2 fresh eggs (uncooked) • a spoon

What to Do:

1 MAKE PREDICTIONS.

Do you think the eggs will float? How might the varying conditions alter the outcome? Record your predictions in your lab notebook.

2 TRY TO FLOAT EGG 1.

Fill one glass half full with water (enough to cover an egg).

Place the egg in the water. Does it float or sink?

TRY TO FLOAT EGG 2.

Pour the same amount of water into a second glass.

Add salt, about one teaspoon at a time. Stir to help it dissolve.

Place the second egg in the water. What happens?

If the egg does not float, keep adding salt. How much salt do you have to add to get your egg to float?

CHEW ON THIS!

Ever notice that it's easier to float in the ocean than in a swimming pool? That's because salt water is denser than fresh water. When you add salt to the water, that dissolved salt adds to the mass of the water without adding much to its volume—so it becomes denser. The more salt you add, the denser the salt water becomes and the easier it is for your egg to rise. The egg in the unsalted water, however, sinks because an egg is denser than fresh water.

DIG DEEPER

ORANGE YOU CURIOUS?

Does an orange float or sink? Put it in a bowl of water and find out. Now peel the orange and try the experiment again. What happens?

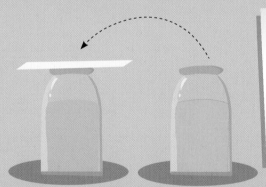

 SAFETY TIPS

- Ask an adult for help with the hot water and stacking the two bottles! You don't want water everywhere!
- Try these activities over a sink to be extra cautious.

HOT AND COLD

Fill a two-liter bottle with cold water and add a few drops of blue food coloring. Fill another bottle with hot tap water and add red food coloring. Cover the top of the cold water bottle with an index card to form a seal. *With help from an adult*, hold the index card in place and quickly turn the covered bottle upside down to fit exactly over the bottle of hot water. Remove the index card. What do you see?

Challenge Points

10

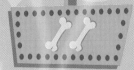

DISAPPEARING ACT

In nature, how does water change from liquid to gas and back again?

What You'll Need:

• a measuring cup • dirt • a large metal or plastic mixing bowl • water • a spoon

• a clear drinking glass (less than half as high as the bowl) • plastic wrap • a marble

What to Do:

1 MAKE YOUR EXPERIMENT.

Pour two cups of dirt and four cups of water into the bowl. Mix thoroughly.

Carefully place the glass in the center of the bowl. Do not let the mixture into it.

Cover the top of the bowl with a sheet of plastic wrap. Make sure the wrap is tight around the bowl's rim but dips slightly in the middle.

Put the bowl in a sunny spot. Rest the marble on the wrap directly above the glass so it weighs the wrap down a bit in the center.

2 OBSERVE AND RECORD.

Watch the bowl to see what happens. After several hours, remove the plastic wrap. What do you notice?

CHEW ON THIS!

After peeling off the wrap, you can see that the dirt is drier and the glass now has clean water inside. That's because the mist that formed on the plastic wrap changed into larger drops of water, which dripped into the glass. Why? The sun warmed the water, making it evaporate (the liquid water turned into water vapor, a gas). The vapor rose, then cooled when it hit the wrap. That made it condense (turn into liquid form) and drip into the glass.

You made a mini version of the water cycle that happens in nature. The sun's heat causes water to evaporate from lakes, oceans, and other bodies of water. Water also evaporates from plants' and trees' leaves, which is called transpiration. When the water reaches cooler air, it condenses into clouds. When the clouds become too heavy with water, they release it as precipitation—rain, snow, or sleet. This is called the water cycle.

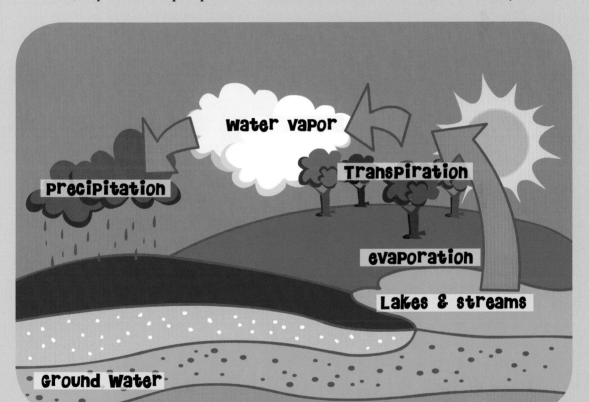

DIG DEEPER

PLANT IN A JAR

Put a well-watered, small potted plant in a large, wide-mouthed jar. Tightly screw the lid on, and leave the jar in a sunny (but not too hot) place for a month. What happens? (After 30 days, remove the plant from the jar so it can get some fresh air.)

WATER MAGIC TRICK

Is it possible to bend water? Maybe.
Here's a trick to astound your friends.

What You'll Need:

• a balloon • a wool hat (optional)

What to Do:

1 PREPARE THE EXPERIMENT.

Blow up the balloon and tie a knot at the end.

Turn on a faucet to run a VERY thin stream of cold water.
Notice how it flows vertically.

Rub the balloon on your hair or a wool hat.

2 BEND WATER!

Slowly bring the balloon close to the thin stream of water—without actually touching it—and prepare to be amazed!

3 OBSERVE AND EXPERIMENT.

How does the distance between the water and the balloon determine how much the water bends?

Adjust the faucet. Does the size of the stream make a difference?

Try using warm water. Does the water's temperature affect how it bends?

Do the experiment in the bathroom sink after someone has taken a shower. Does humidity change your results?

WATER MAGIC TRICK

VARIABLE	EFFECT
THIN COLD STREAM	
DISTANCE	
SIZE OF STREAM	
WATER TEMPERATURE	
HUMIDITY IN ROOM	

CHEW ON THIS!

Did you really make magic? No, but you did make static electricity! Static electricity is the same force that makes your hair stand up after you take off your winter hat. In this experiment, you gave the balloon a static charge, and the charged balloon made the water move toward it.

By rubbing the balloon on your hair, tiny particles from your hair, called electrons, collected on the balloon. These electrons have a negative charge. Water is also made up of charged particles. Since opposites attract, the particles in the water move around so that the positively charged particles of the water are closer to the negatively charged particles of the balloon. This attraction was strong enough to pull the flowing water toward the balloon.

DIG DEEPER

STATIC CLING

Rub a balloon against your clothes and see if it sticks to a wall. Did it work?

MOTION COMMOTION

You'd think a big celebrity like me would have some kind of flashy car. But no, the only things this dog uses to get from place to place are four paws and a leash. Still, there was that one time I made a doghouse submarine and took it to Australia. Maybe you can make the perfect vehicle for me to get around town in. I have things to do, places to be. Like that hip-and-happening hydrant where Charlene hangs out.

ALL WOUND UP

Power a race car with a rubber band? Yup! Wind it up and then let it zip across the floor. But try not to get a speeding ticket. Ready, set, roll!

What You'll Need:

• a large spool (at least 1¼ inch in diameter) • a rubber band (just a little longer than the spool's height) • a drinking straw (or a pencil or toothpick) • a small paper clip (shorter than the spool's diameter) • masking tape • a metal washer (1 inch or less in diameter works best)

What to Do:

1 BUILD YOUR RACER.

Slip the rubber band through the center of the spool. If it gets stuck, use the straw to push it through.

Slide the paper clip through one loop of the rubber band. Tape it down.

Pull the other end of the rubber band through the washer. Then slide the straw through the rubber-band loop.

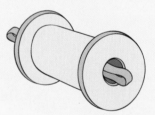

2 ENERGIZE YOUR RACER.
At first, the rubber band may be so loose that the straw slips out. Wind up the straw twenty times or so. The rubber band will get tighter and pull everything together.

3 LAUNCH YOUR RACER.
Put the racer on the floor or a tabletop and let it go. Does it move in a straight line? Does it spin? Adjust the racer's parts to make it move the way you want.

4 RACE YOUR FRIENDS.
Test whose racer goes the fastest, farthest, or straightest. Try it on a rug. How do different surfaces affect the way the racer moves?

CHEW ON THIS!

When you wind up the rubber band, you store energy in it. As the rubber band unwinds, this stored energy (called potential energy) changes into energy of motion (called kinetic energy). The more potential energy that gets turned into kinetic energy, the farther and faster your racer will go. Notice that when the straw tries to spin, it hits the table, which stops it from turning. But the other end of the rubber band (attached to the paper clip) can spin freely. When it unwinds, it pushes on the spool, making it spin.

DIG DEEPER

HIT A TARGET
Make a target, such as a crumpled ball of paper. Wind up your racer, set it two feet away from the target, aim, and try to hit your target. How can you make your racer drive straight every time?

CLIMB A HILL
Make a ramp from a piece of cardboard. Set your racer at the bottom and see if it can climb to the top. Experiment with gentle and steep ramps. How can you improve your racer's traction and power?

PUSH A BALL
Set a small, light ball, such as a Ping-Pong ball, in front of your racer. See how far it can push the ball.

BLAST OFF!

Use air power to send a straw
rocket flying high!

SAFETY TIP

• Always point your rocket
  away from people before
  launching it.

What You'll Need:

• an empty 20-ounce plastic bottle • a thin straw • clay or poster putty • a wide straw
(that fits over the thin straw)

What to Do:

1 BUILD A ROCKET LAUNCHER.

Hold the thin straw about an inch down into the mouth of the bottle.

Wrap a ball of clay about the size of a quarter around the bottle opening, sealing it
tightly around the straw and the bottle so no air can escape.

Now squeeze the bottle. Do you feel air coming out of the top of the straw?

2 BUILD A ROCKET.

Seal up one end of the wide straw with a small ball of clay to form your rocket.
Place the open end of the wide straw over the thinner straw on the rocket launcher.

3 BLAST OFF!

Wrap both hands around the bottle and squeeze firmly. Your rocket should fly through the air. If the rocket doesn't launch, practice squeezing the bottle harder and check that there are no holes in the clay.

4 DESIGN MORE ROCKETS.

Make different rockets by attaching wings and tails to other wide straws. Use construction paper, string, or bits of streamers. Test the rockets. Which ones flew the farthest? Did any curve in the air? How did your additions change the way they flew?

CHEW ON THIS!

When you squeeze the plastic bottle, the air inside the bottle pushes through both straws. Since the top of the wide straw is plugged up, the air has no place to escape, so the air pressure launches the straw into the air.

DIG DEEPER

TAKE IT OUTSIDE
Make wings or tails for your rockets from leaves, grass, or other materials found in nature.

BALLOON RACER
Can you get a balloon to shoot across a room on a zip line? Get a straw, some string, some tape, and a balloon. Thread the string through the straw, and ask two friends to hold each end of the string. Blow up the balloon, and hold it closed. Tape the balloon to the straw. Release the balloon, and see what happens!

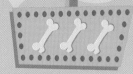

BLOW IT AWAY

A wind-powered car? Yes. It's a little bit car and a little bit sailboat. Build a car and use the wind to move it.

What You'll Need:

• 2 drinking straws • a 4" x 6" index card • 4 hard mint candies with holes in the middle
• 2–4 paper cups • a plastic bag • rubber bands • tape • string • 15–20 paper clips • a ruler
• scissors • a sheet of paper • an electric fan

What to Do:

1 BUILD YOUR CAR.

Assemble the car body and wheels as shown.

Tape the straws to the underside of the index card.

Slip a candy onto each end of the straws, and tape the straw edges to keep the wheels on.

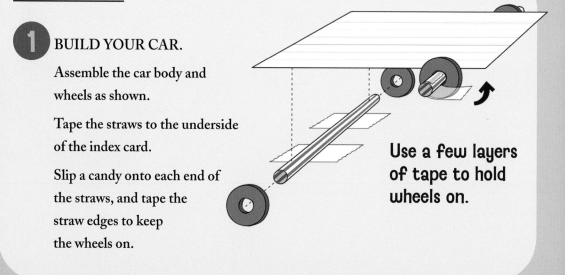

Use a few layers of tape to hold wheels on.

DESIGN A WIND CATCHER.

Brainstorm some ways to modify your car to capture the wind to make it move.

3 BUILD YOUR WIND CATCHER.

Choose one of your ideas. Build your system and add it to your car.

4 ATTACH A LOAD.

Tie ten paper clips together with string. Tape the free end of the string to the back of the car so that the paper clips trail an inch or two behind the car. These paper clips are your load. Adding them to your car makes it a bigger challenge—you have to catch a lot of wind to make your loaded car move!

5 TEST AND REDESIGN.

Mark a finish line two feet from the fan. Set your car and paper clips next to the fan. Turn the fan on low speed. (You may need to aim the fan so the wind hits your wind catcher.) Did your car pull the paper clips across the finish line? If not, make a change and try again. If your car was successful, try the Dig Deeper challenges.

CHEW ON THIS!

The wind from the fan applies a force to your wind catcher. Since the wind catcher is attached to the car, this force from the wind moves the car. The more wind you catch, the faster your car goes. You can also help your car go faster by getting the wheels to roll smoothly and evenly (that is, by reducing friction). The more friction there is, the more force it takes to move the car.

DIG DEEPER

DO A MONSTER TRUCK PULL
How many paper clips can your car pull?
Add five at a time.

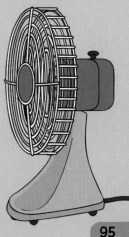

PUT YOUR BREEZE MOBILE TO THE TEST
Can your car cross a finish line that's
three feet away from the fan? Four feet?

FLOAT MY BOAT

Build aluminum-foil boats and test different
designs to see how many pennies
you can load without sinking
your boat. Let's dive in!

Oh, no! I was filling the tub and fell
asleep! Now my doghouse is flooded!
Can you design a boat to carry as much
of my stuff as possible?

What You'll Need:

• 6-inch squares of aluminum foil • ruler • a container half-filled with water • pennies

What to Do:

1 ROUND 1: BUILD BOATS.

Make a boat by bending the foil. Draw your design in your lab notebook,
and label the side height and the bottom length and width.

2 MAKE A PREDICTION.

In your lab notebook, enter your prediction for how many pennies your
boat can hold before it sinks.

3 TEST THE DESIGN.

Float your boat. Add pennies one at a time. Keep going until the boat sinks.
Count how many pennies your boat held. But don't count the last one—it sank
the boat!

Enter this number in your lab notebook.

Repeat steps 2–4, making a total of three boats.

4 ROUND 2: BUILD MORE BOATS.

Make new designs using what you learned about the height and thickness of the sides, the size of the bottom, and how to position the pennies. Record your designs, predictions, and test results in your lab notebook.

CHEW ON THIS!

When a boat floats, it settles into the water, pushing the water aside to make room for itself. But it's a two-way pushing match — the water pushes back on the bottom and sides of the boat. This force, called buoyancy, holds the boat up. The more water a boat pushes aside, the more force there will be pushing back on the boat and supporting it. This is why a boat's size and shape make such a difference in how much of a load it can carry without sinking.

DIG DEEPER

Ready to "sink" your teeth into a few more challenges?

CARGO SHIP?

Can a really big foil boat carry a lot of pennies? Build several boats using 12-inch squares of foil. How many pennies does it take to sink these boats?

LAKE OR OCEAN

Does the kind of water you float a boat in make a difference? Test to discover if your boat holds more pennies when it floats in fresh water or in salt water. To make salt water, dissolve two cups of salt in a gallon of warm tap water.

Great work! Things will be back to normal just as soon as I wring out my bark-o-lounger!

Science Fair Tip

Display your designs (initial and revised) on your presentation board. Include your boat's measurements, as well as how many pennies each design actually carried without sinking.

Challenge Points

10

HANG TIME

Time to drop everything. Really! Build some copters and race them. The winner hits the ground LAST. Look out below!

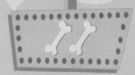

No, really –
LOOK OUT!

What You'll Need:

• a few sheets of paper • scissors • paper clips (1 large and 1 small)

What to Do:

1 MAKE YOUR COPTER.

Photocopy or trace the copter on page 99.
Cut along the dotted lines.
Assemble it as shown.

2 LAUNCH YOUR COPTER.

Hold your copter as high as you can.
Let go and watch as it falls.
Does it spin to the ground?

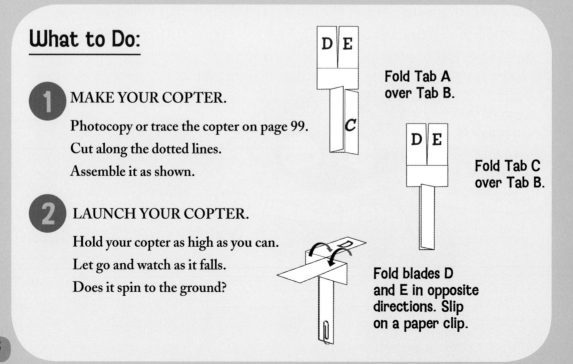

Fold Tab A
over Tab B.

Fold Tab C
over Tab B.

Fold blades D
and E in opposite
directions. Slip
on a paper clip.

3 CHANGE YOUR COPTER.

Build a second copter of your own design. This time, change a feature, such as the copter's size or the shape of the blades. Try using more or fewer paper clips. Then launch both the new and original copter designs and compare how they fall. What kind of difference did your change make?

CHEW ON THIS!

When you drop your copter, its blades hit the air. The air pushes back on the blades, giving each one a little push forward. Notice how the blades are not exactly across from each other. This means that one blade is nudging one side of the copter around while the other blade is nudging the other side around. These two pushes work together to spin the copter around its center point. The spinning blades hit a lot of air on the way down, and all this air pushes back on the blades. The more air you can get to hit your blades (that is, the more push-back you can create), the slower your copter will fall.

DIG DEEPER

WHAT SIZE?

Experiment with the size of your copter. How big or small can you make it and still have it spin as it falls to the ground?

WHICH WAY IS UP?

Does your copter always spin in the same direction? Mark one blade with a bold color. Then watch as your copter falls to the ground. Now figure out how to make it spin in the opposite direction.

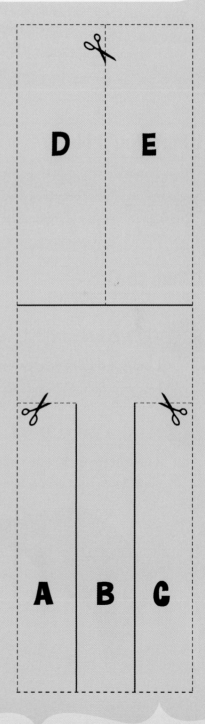

D E

A B C

SKYDIVER

Design a parachute that floats safely to the ground—no crash landings allowed!

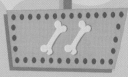

Chet's last hobby was fire ant juggling – he lost a few whiskers in that experiment! Now he wants to try skydiving, and there's no stopping him! Can you design a parachute to keep my little buddy safe?

What You'll Need:

• 10-inch squares of: lightweight plastic (like clear bags from the grocery store), heavy-weight plastic (like thick trash bags), tissue paper, and notebook or copier paper
• 8-inch pieces of string or thread (4 per parachute) • scissors • large paper clips

What to Do:

1 TEST YOUR MATERIALS.

Compare the different types of materials, and pick the one you think will make the best parachute. What are some tests you can do to decide which material to use?

2 MAKE A PARACHUTE.

Tie string to each corner of the parachute, taking care to keep the string lengths even. Then tie the ends together around a large paper clip.

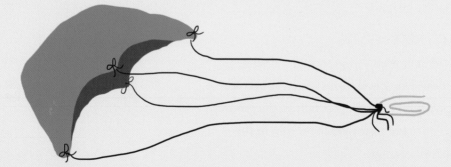

3 FLOAT IT.

Hold up your parachute and drop it. What happens as it falls to the ground?

4 DESIGN AND TEST ANOTHER PARACHUTE.

Select a different material and make another parachute. Compare how it falls with the parachute you made earlier.

5 MAKE IT BIG!

Make a parachute at least double the size of the others you made. What adjustments do you need to make to get the bigger parachute to work?

CHEW ON THIS!

When you throw something into the air, it falls because gravity pulls it to the ground. As a parachute falls, the part that fills with air is called the canopy. A parachute works because air gets trapped in the canopy and slows its fall. This is the result of air resistance, the force of the air against the canopy.

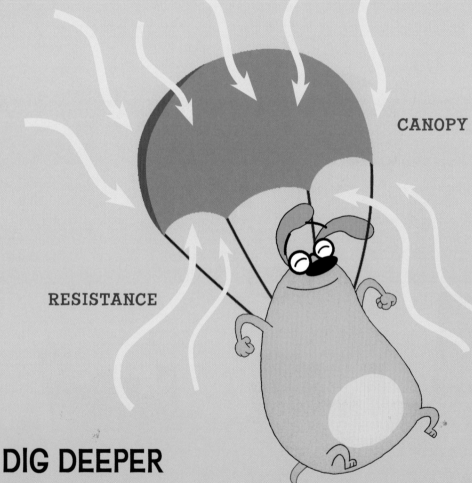

GRAVITY PUSHES DOWN

CANOPY

RESISTANCE

DIG DEEPER

TAKE IT OUTSIDE

Test your parachute on a windy day. What difference does the wind make?

SUPER-SIZE IT!

Can you make a really big parachute — so big, it's super-size? Using what you know about making a parachute, make one that's big enough to float safely when dropped from a significant height, like in an open stairwell or out a window. If necessary, get permission first before dropping your extra-large parachute!

DOGGY EARS

Not to brag or anything, but do you know that dogs can hear about four times the distance of a human who has normal hearing? All the better to listen to my peppy, toe-tapping theme song, my honking novelty pencil, and my singing voice in the shower—mostly show tunes at a high volume. (I used to play accordion in there, too, but the shampoo clogged up all the keys.) Try making these sound machines. I'm all ears!

BOTTLE KARAOKE

Make music and science!
Blow into bottles to create
different vibrations
and play a song.

WARNING:
Ruff might sing along.

What You'll Need:

• 5–8 identical plastic bottles • water • food coloring (optional)

What to Do:

1 MAKE YOUR BOTTLE FLUTES.

Fill the bottles with different levels of water, but don't fill any to the top. You can add food coloring to make the levels easier to see.

2 PLAY A TUNE.

Gently blow across the top of each bottle until you hear a note.

Listen to the sound each bottle makes. Do different levels of water make different notes? If so, arrange the bottles from lowest to highest note. Can you play a song?

3 OBSERVE AND RECORD.

Compare the notes the bottles make. Then draw a picture of your bottle flutes in your lab notebook and record your findings.

CHEW ON THIS!

Blowing across each bottle makes the air inside vibrate, producing a note. Different vibrations make different notes. The amount of air and water in each bottle affects its sound. The bottles with more air create slower vibrations and low notes, and the bottles with less air create faster vibrations and high notes. That's why when you add water, the notes get higher.

More air produces slower vibration and lower notes

The sine waves shown here represent pitch and frequency of vibrations. When they are farther apart, lower notes result. When they are closer together, higher notes result.

Less air creates quicker vibration and higher notes

DIG DEEPER

MUSIC IS EVERYWHERE

Flick each bottle with your finger. What do you hear? Experiment by flicking an empty bottle or tapping one with ice cubes in it. Compare the sounds. Explore more sound waves by tapping other objects around your house.

RUBBER-BAND GUITAR

Make your own guitar by stretching rubber bands of the same length, but different thicknesses, around a lidless shoe box. Pluck them to make notes. Does a rubber band's thickness affect the sound it makes? Next try varying lengths instead.

SCREAMING STRING THING

What a racket! Turn an ordinary cup and string into a screeching, squawking sound machine.

What You'll Need:

• a paper or plastic cup • a sharpened pencil • cotton string • scissors • a large paper clip
• tape • water • dish-washing liquid

What to Do:

1 CONSTRUCT YOUR CUP.

Poke a small hole in the bottom of the cup with a pencil.

Pull a string (about two feet long) through the bottom of the cup.

Tie a paper clip to the end that's inside the cup.

Pull the string tight, so that the paper clip rests against the bottom of the cup.

Tape the paper clip flat.

2 MAKE SOME NOISE!

Hold the cup in one hand and the string in the other, near the bottom of the cup.

Squeeze the string tightly between your fingers and thumb, and slide them down the string as fast as you can. What happens?

Now wet the string with water, and slide your fingers along it again. What do you hear?

3 PREDICT, TEST, AND OBSERVE.

Predict what would happen if you put dish-washing liquid on the string. Then test it. Which makes the loudest sound — the dry, wet, or soapy string? Why might one work better than the others?

CHEW ON THIS!

Sound vibrations travel through liquids, gases (like air), and solids (like the string in this activity). Sliding your fingers along the string creates friction (rubbing and sticking). This causes the string to vibrate. The vibrations travel up the string to the cup, which acts like a speaker and amplifies them (makes them sound louder).

But why does the wet string work better than the dry string? The wet string makes your fingers stick and rub more, causing more vibrations and more sound. Why doesn't the soapy string work? The soap is a lubricant. It reduces friction and makes your fingers glide smoothly, causing fewer vibrations and less sound.

DIG DEEPER

LONG-DISTANCE CALL

Get a partner and tie the ends of your two Screaming String Things together to make

a string telephone. Pull the string tight while one person talks into one cup and the other person listens through the other cup. Make another phone with longer string and try making a long-distance call!

HEARING IS BELIEVING!

You'll be amazed by the sounds an ordinary wire coat hanger can make. Tie a piece of string to each corner of a coat hanger. Loop the string around your index fingers. Swing the hanger so it taps against the side of a table. What do you hear?

Tie the strings to your index fingers and put them gently in your ears. Tap the hanger again. Now what do you hear?

WHAT'S THE BUZZ?

Make an instrument that anyone can play — a kazoo — and get the buzz on sound vibrations!

Blossom's relatives, the distinguished von Yum Yum family, invited me to perform in their music recital. Quick! I need an easy instrument that I can learn to play fast. I want to show those MEW-sical felines just what this dog can do!

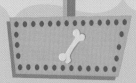

What You'll Need:

• a sharpened pencil • toilet-paper tubes • scissors • waxed paper • rubber bands
• aluminum foil • plastic wrap

What to Do:

1 MAKE A KAZOO.

Use the pencil to make a small hole about two inches from one end of a toilet-paper tube.

Cut a square of waxed paper that's an inch or two wider than the end of the tube.

Wrap the waxed paper tightly over the end of the tube where you made the hole. Hold it in place with a rubber band, making sure you don't cover the hole you made. Trim off any excess waxed paper with scissors. This is your kazoo.

2 PLAY IT!

Place the open end of the kazoo lightly over your mouth and say, "AAHHH!" What happens? Now sing or hum a tune into it. Try making different kinds of sounds to see what causes the loudest buzzing.

3 EXPERIMENT.

Touch the waxed paper with your finger while you play the kazoo. What do you notice?

Cover the hole with your finger while you play the kazoo. What happens? Does the hole make it easier or harder to play it? Why?

Make more kazoos, changing one thing (called a variable). Instead of waxed paper, try aluminum foil or plastic wrap. Predict which material you think will make the best sound. Test it out. Were your predictions right?

4 RECORD YOUR OBSERVATIONS.

ALUMINUM FOIL

WAXED PAPER

CHEW ON THIS!

All sound is made up of vibrations (rapid back-and-forth movements), which produce sound waves that travel through the air to our ears. When you play a kazoo, air carries the sound waves from your mouth down the tube, making the waxed paper vibrate. You can feel those vibrations if you touch the waxed paper.

DIG DEEPER

GET TICKLED

Fold a piece of waxed paper in half and wrap it around the teeth of a comb. Put your lips lightly against the comb and hum. How do your lips feel? Who knew sound vibrations could feel so funny?

MAKE A STRAW KAZOO

Flatten one end of a straw by biting on it. Then cut the flattened end into an upside-down V shape. To make music, place the V end of the straw in your mouth, just past the inside of your lips. Press on the V with your lips while blowing. To experiment, cut the straw and then blow on it. Hear a difference?

WHO LET THE DOG OUT?

Henry, my boss, has been hounding me to do more physical activity. It's all because I got stuck in a bee costume during a show. Man, that was a buzzkill. But, hey, it wasn't my fault. The zipper was broken. Honest!

Still, it couldn't hurt to take this dog for a walk. Let's get outside and do some nature-based activities. Like catching a cloud in a jar, making our own stalactite, and sending a potato through a maze — you know, just your usual, everyday nature stuff.

THE WORM SHOW

Introducing the stars of your garden — the amazing worms! Make your own wormery and see how worms help plants grow.

Look at that worm boogie! This little guy belongs at Chet's freeze dance parties!

What You'll Need:

• a large plastic bottle • scissors • soil • sand • dead leaves • water • earthworms
• plastic wrap • a pencil • black construction paper • tape

What to Do:

1 MAKE YOUR WORMERY.

Cut the top off the plastic bottle.

Fill the bottle with alternating layers of soil and sand.
Add dead leaves and four teaspoons of water.

Go outside and look under piles of dead leaves or dig in the dirt to find two to five earthworms. Gently set them in your wormery.

Cover the top of the bottle with plastic wrap, and poke air holes in it with the pencil.

Draw a picture of the wormery in your lab notebook. This is your "before" picture.

Wrap the bottle in black construction paper, and tape it in place.

② MAINTAIN YOUR WORMERY IN A COOL LOCATION.

Every day, add a couple teaspoons of water to keep the soil moist but not wet. Remove the black paper after two weeks.

③ OBSERVE AND RECORD WHAT HAPPENED.

Draw an "after" picture in your lab notebook of what happened.

Applaud the worms for their spectacular show, then return the contents of the entire wormery (worms, too!) back outside to their original home.

CHEW ON THIS!

The separate layers of soil and sand become all mixed together. Why? The wiggling worms mix them up as they make tunnels. These tunnels help bring air and water down to the roots of your plants. Worms also break down dead leaves and plant waste and fertilize the soil. This brings nutrients down to the roots of your plants. So if your garden is growing, thank the worms!

DIG DEEPER

BREAK IT DOWN

You can make a bigger wormery using a large fish tank. This time, add a few objects — some that you predict are biodegradable, or capable of being decomposed by bacteria or other living organisms, and some that you think are not. Which objects break down and which ones don't?

Science Fair Tip

Expand this experiment with the "Break It Down" Dig Deeper challenge. Take "before" and "after" photos, and post them on your presentation board.

WORM FARM

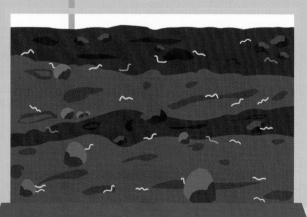

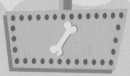

CLOUD IN A JAR

Can you create a cloud in a jar? Give it a try with this nifty meteorology experiment!

SAFETY TIPS

- Ask an adult for help!
- Keep the aerosol spray away from your eyes, nose, and mouth. No inhaling or tasting!
- Have an adult help you heat and pour the water.

What You'll Need:

• a small, clean glass jar with a lid • water • a teakettle • an oven mitt • ice cubes
• an aerosol can, such as hairspray or air freshener • black paper • a flashlight (optional)

What to Do:

1 PREPARE THE JAR.

Ask an adult to heat (but NOT boil) some water in a teakettle and pour an inch of the hot water into your jar.

Then ask the adult to wear the oven mitt and swirl the hot water around the sides of the jar to warm up the glass.

2 SET UP THE ICE.

Flip the jar lid upside down to use as a container, and place the ice cubes in it.

Rest the upside-down lid of ice on top of the jar for three seconds.

3 MAKE A CLOUD.

Lift the lid full of ice, and quickly spray a small burst of aerosol into the jar.

Return the lid of ice to the top of the jar.

OBSERVE AND RECORD.

Place the black paper behind the jar and watch what happens.

Shine a flashlight into the jar to observe it more closely.

Remove the lid and touch the cloud.

Record your observations in your lab notebook.

CHEW ON THIS!

When you pour the hot water into the jar, you trap it to create warm, moist air. Some of the water evaporates into water vapor. As that warm air containing water vapor rises in the jar, the ice on top cools it. Cool air can't hold as much water vapor as warm air, so this excess vapor collects around the floating aerosol particles, making your cloud! This process is known as condensation.

Clouds in the sky are created in a similar way. They form when warm air rises, expands, and then cools. Some of the vapor condenses onto dust and other tiny floating particles. When billions of these droplets come together, they form a cloud.

DIG DEEPER

NAME THAT CLOUD

There are four main types of clouds—cumulus (puffy), stratus (long, flat, and low), cirrus (thin and wispy), and nimbus (rainy). See if you can identify these clouds in the sky. Draw them in your lab notebook.

CIRRUS

CUMULUS

STRATUS

NIMBUS

INSTANT RAINBOW

All you need to make a rainbow is a garden hose and a sunny day. With your back to the sun, spray a fine mist of water against a dark background, such as your lawn or driveway. Can you see the rainbow?

15

MAKE YOUR OWN STALACTITE

It can take up to 4,000 years for a stalactite to grow one inch! But you can make one in a week.

Four thousand YEARS? Egad! That's 28,000 years in dog years! We don't have that kind of time, FETCHers. I better stop yapping so you can get started. . . .

What You'll Need:

• a mixing bowl • water • a measuring cup • a spoon • a box of Epsom salts (found at the drugstore) • paper clips • 2 feet of cotton string • 2 glasses • waxed paper • a saucer

What to Do:

1 START YOUR STALACTITE (AND STALAGMITE).

Fill the bowl with 2 cups of warm water. Stir in 1 cup of Epsom salts until you can't dissolve any more. (It's OK if not all of the salt dissolves.)

Fill each glass with half of the solution, and position them about a foot apart on a piece of waxed paper.

Tie paper clips to both ends of the string.

Dip an end of the string in each glass with the paper clips inside them. Let the middle of the string hang between the two glasses. Place the saucer underneath to catch the drips.

Set aside for a week or longer.

2 OBSERVE AND RECORD.

Watch what happens over the next week. Write down and draw what you see in your lab notebook.

CHEW ON THIS!

The Epsom salt solution traveled along the string until it reached the middle, where it dripped onto the saucer. Over a few days, the dripping water evaporated and left behind the Epsom salt, forming a tiny stalactite and stalagmite (icicle-shaped columns of rock-hard minerals found in underground caves). Stalactites hang from above, while stalagmites build up from the ground.

A stalactite forms when rainwater dissolves a mineral called calcite and then drips from a cave's roof. Each drop leaves behind a tiny bit of the calcite. Over a VERY long period of time, the hardened calcite accumulates into a stalactite. Stalagmites form when the calcite drips to the ground and gradually grows up from the floor.

DIG DEEPER

WAIT A WEEK

Set your stalactite aside for more than a week. Will your stalactite and stalagmite meet and grow together as a column?

OTHER INGREDIENTS

Instead of Epsom salt, use other substances, such as baking soda, table salt, or sugar. Do you get the same results? Why or why not?

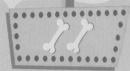

THE A-MAZE-ING SPUD

Can a potato escape a maze? Try this eye-opening experiment and see for yourself!

I often act like a potato – a couch potato! Ahh. It's time to watch a little *FETCH!*

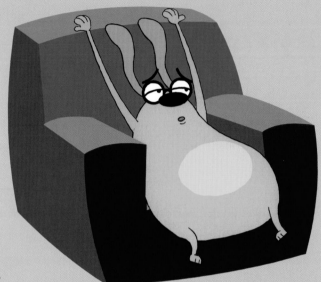

What You'll Need:

• a sprouting potato • a large shoe box with a lid • a small flowerpot that will fit in your shoe box • potting soil • water • scissors • pieces of cardboard • tape

What to Do:

1   PREPARE YOUR POTATO.
Plant the potato in a flowerpot filled with moist soil. Leave ¾ inch of the potato and a sprout above the soil.

2 MAKE YOUR MAZE.

Cut a small hole, about the size of a quarter, on a short end of the shoe box.

Put the potted potato in the opposite end of the box.

Create the maze's walls by taping cardboard pieces to the bottom of the box. Make sure to leave gaps in the walls for the potato shoots to sprout through.

Put the lid on the box, and place it by a sunny window. Don't touch it for a month.

3 OBSERVE AND RECORD.

After four weeks, open the box. What do you see? What color is the potato shoot?

CHEW ON THIS!

Why do potatoes sometimes sprout in your cupboard? For the same reason the potato shoot made its way through the maze and reached the hole at the end of the box. Plants have cells that are sensitive to light and indicate to the plant which way to grow. That's how the potato shoot made its way through the maze to reach the light at the end. Plants turn energy from the sun into food energy, so they always grow toward the light even if they are buried in deep soil.

The shoot is white instead of green because if plants don't get enough sunlight, they can't make chlorophyll, the chemical that makes them green.

DIG DEEPER

GREEN MACHINE

See how sunlight affects a plant's cholorophyll by sandwiching one of a plant's leaves between two pieces of black paper. After a week, remove the paper. What happened?

119

WHICH WAY TO THE NORTH POLE?

See how magnets work by making your own compass.

SAFETY TIPS

- Ask an adult for help.
- Be careful with that needle!

What You'll Need:

• a bowl • water • dish-washing liquid • a big needle • a strong magnet (found at a hardware store) • a ¼-inch piece of cork or thin sheet of paper cut into a circle (use the bottom of a drinking glass to trace one)

What to Do:

1 MAKE YOUR COMPASS.

Fill a bowl with water. Add a dab of dish-washing liquid.

Magnetize the needle by stroking it 20 times *in the same direction* from its eye to its point with one end of the magnet.

Carefully poke the needle through the cork or thread it through the circular paper.

Float the cork or paper in the middle of the bowl. What do you see? (Be patient. It may take a little while for something to happen.)

2 TEST YOUR COMPASS.

Turn the paper back to its original position. Which way does the needle spin? Compare the direction with a real compass.

CHEW ON THIS!

Your compass needle should always point north. To discover why, you need to know how magnets work. Magnets pull, or attract, other magnets and some metals, such as iron. Every magnet has two poles, areas where its force is the strongest—a north pole and a south pole. Opposite poles of magnets attract each other, while the same poles push away, or repel, one another.

Your needle is made of steel, which contains jumbled-up particles of iron. By stroking it with a magnet, you made these particles all face the same way, thus magnetizing the needle.

The inside of our planet has so much iron that it's like one giant magnet. Your compass's needle lines up with the earth's magnetic field, so no matter where you are, it will always point toward the North Pole.

DIG DEEPER

MAGNET SCAVENGER HUNT

Go around the house seeing how many objects you can find that are attracted to your magnet. Draw pictures of each object, take a photo, or make a video of the magnet at work.

MAGNETIC CAR RACE

Race a car without even touching it! Draw a racetrack on a large cardboard sheet. Then attach a strong magnet to the bottom of a lightweight toy car. Put the car on the track. To race it, hold another magnet under the car and move it around the track. Make a second magnetic car to race a buddy.

TRIUMPH TALLY

Thanks for playing with Ruff! If you're here, you're ready to add up your Challenge Points for a Triumph Tally. Check your score against the ratings scale below to see how you did. Good luck!

IF YOU SCORED BETWEEN 154 AND 307, YOU'RE A SCIENTIST!

IF YOU SCORED BETWEEN 20 AND 153, YOU'RE A LAB ASSISTANT!

Good work, FETCHer! You've completed some experiments and learned a lot about how things work. Keep experimenting, observing, and recording, and you're well on your way to becoming a Science Superstar! I'd tip my hat to you, but I'm not wearing one.

Hot diggety dog! You've finished more than half of my experiments! Your accomplishment proves that you're a hard worker, persistent, and curious – all traits of a good scientist. The world needs scientists like you to help care for our earth and those who live on it. And personally, I need someone to invent a refrigerator door that dogs can open by themselves. Hint, hint.

IF YOU SCORED BETWEEN 308 AND 460, YOU'RE A SCIENCE SUPERSTAR!

Hear that noise? It's the sound of Blossom, Chet, and me giving you a standing ovation. Take a bow, Science Superstar. You're the Grand FETCHer Champion! You've won a . . . well, I don't have the prize on me, but you get a snazzy Certificate of Completion (see page 125). Now that you've mastered most – or all – of the science experiments in this book, try creating your own. Who knows? You might discover the world's next scientific breakthrough!

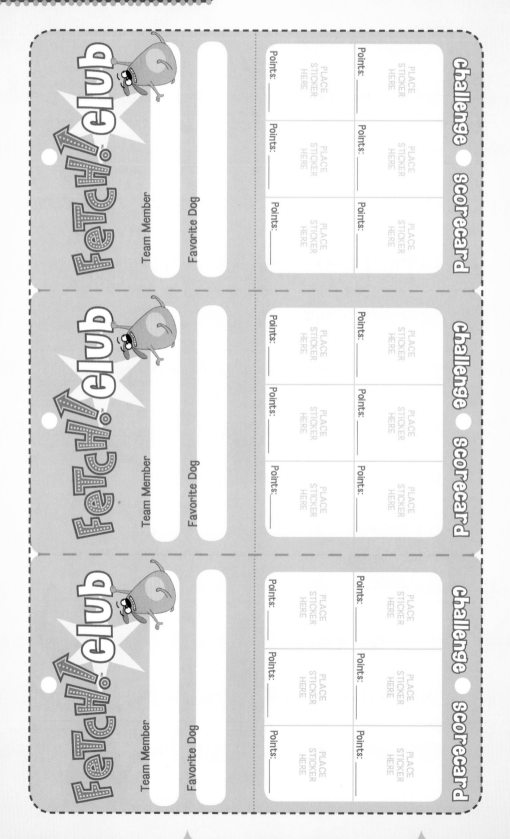

Fetch! Club

Team Member

Favorite Dog

Challenge ● scorecard

PLACE STICKER HERE
Points: _____

PLACE STICKER HERE
Points: _____

PLACE STICKER HERE
Points: _____

Fetch! Club

Team Member

Favorite Dog

Challenge ● scorecard

PLACE STICKER HERE
Points: _____

PLACE STICKER HERE
Points: _____

PLACE STICKER HERE
Points: _____

PLACE STICKER HERE
Points: _____

PLACE STICKER HERE
Points: _____

Fetch! Club

Team Member

Favorite Dog

Challenge ● scorecard

PLACE STICKER HERE
Points: _____

PLACE STICKER HERE
Points: _____

PLACE STICKER HERE
Points: _____

PLACE STICKER HERE
Points: _____

FETCH! with Ruff Ruffman™

PBS KIDS GO!

courageous

Determined

curious

Bold

Fun

Daring

Congratulates

For doing a fantastic job on your challenges at the FETCH! club.
You're talented, brilliant, and totally awesome!!!

Ruff

Your Fabulous Canine Host

Fearless

Cooperative

Much like Ruff, many of the materials needed for the activities in this book can be found lying around the doghouse. As the show supervisor, Blossom doesn't like to leave anyone hanging. So, she compiled these lists of materials that are a bit harder to come by. Happy FETCHing!

STUFF YOU CAN FIND AT THE GROCERY STORE

Baker's yeast
Baking powder
Baking soda
Cola
Cranberry juice
Dog biscuits (large)
Food coloring
Grape juice concentrate
Lemon juice
Mini marshmallows
Purple grape juice
Vanilla extract
Whipping cream
White vinegar
Wintergreen-flavored
   hard candies made
   with wintergreen oil

Be sure you have all of the required materials before you start an experiment!

STUFF YOU CAN FIND AT A HARDWARE STORE

Foam pipe insulation tubing
   (¾ inch or 1 inch in diameter)
Flowerpot, small
Potted plants (three, all the
   same size and type)
Potting soil
Metal washers
Magnet (strong)
Silicone spray lubricant

STUFF YOU MAY BE ABLE TO FIND OUTSIDE

Dirt
Earthworms
Leaves (dead)
Sand
Soil

STUFF YOU CAN FIND AT A CRAFTS STORE

Balloons
Craft sticks
Straws (various widths)
Sand (clean)
Spool (large: at least 1¼ inch in diameter)

STUFF YOU CAN FIND AT AN OFFICE-SUPPLY STORE

Brass fasteners
Chart paper
Clay or poster putty
Cork sheet (¼" thick)
Cups (both plastic and paper—unwaxed)
Index cards
Transparency film, 8" x 11" (for overhead projectors)

STUFF YOU CAN FIND AT A DRUGSTORE

Iodine
Pipettes or eyedroppers
pH strips*

*pH paper strips are sometimes found at drugstores and are also found at some health food stores and aquarium or pool-supply stores.

Copyright © 2015 by WGBH Educational Foundation. The PBS KIDS logo is a registered mark of PBS and is used with permission. Major funding for *Fetch!* is provided by the National Science Foundation and public television viewers. This *Fetch!* material is based upon work supported by the National Science Foundation under Grant No. 0813513. Any opinions, findings, and conclusions or recommendations expressed in this material are those of the author(s) and do not necessarily reflect the views of the National Science Foundation. All rights reserved. No part of this book may be reproduced, transmitted, or stored in an information retrieval system in any form or by any means, graphic, electronic, or mechanical, including photocopying, taping, and recording, without prior written permission from the publisher. First edition 2015. Library of Congress Catalog Card Number 2013953461. ISBN 978-0-7636-7432-8. This book was typeset in Adobe Caslon Semibold. The illustrations were created digitally. Candlewick Entertainment, an imprint of Candlewick Press. 99 Dover Street, Somerville, Massachusetts 02144. visit us at www.candlewick.com. Printed in Humen, Dongguan, China. 14 15 16 17 18 19 SCP 10 9 8 7 6 5 4 3 2 1

INDEX (BY SUBJECT)